Greek
and Roman
Jewellery

Greek and Roman Jewellery

Filippo Coarelli

HAMLYN

Translated by Dr D. Strong from the Italian original

L'oreficeria nell'arte classica

© *1966 Fratelli Fabbri Editori, Milan*

This edition © *copyright 1970*
THE HAMLYN PUBLISHING GROUP LIMITED
LONDON · NEW YORK · SYDNEY · TORONTO
Hamlyn House, Feltham, Middlesex, England

ISBN 0 600 01247 6

Text filmset by Filmtype Services, Scarborough, England

Printed in Italy by Fratelli Fabbri Editori, Milan

Bound in Scotland by Hunter and Foulis Ltd., Edinburgh

Contents

INTRODUCTION

Interest in Classical jewellery is a fairly recent phenomenon as far as the art historian and the archaeologist are concerned. Among antiquarians and collectors, of course, there has always been a keen interest in the subject; ever since the Renaissance, collections of ancient gold and gems have been formed and, in many cases, these have become the nucleus of the treasures of the big modern museums. Much earlier still, the Hellenistic kings and the Roman patricians of the Republic made similar collections, as Pliny the Elder records.

Excavation, which provides the raw material of archaeological research, is often thought of by the general public as nothing more than a treasure-hunt, and in popular books on archaeology the spectacular discoveries which apparently confirm this myth – the 'Treasure of Priam' is a good example – are given a very important place. But despite the immense popularity of gold, it is only in the last few decades that there has been any scientific study of ancient jewellery. This is partly due to an old prejudice, which divided the arts into 'major' and 'minor'; this was not an ancient prejudice, since in Hellenistic and Roman times the 'toreutist' (that is to say, the maker of silver relief-work) could become as famous as the painter or sculptor. Mentor and Mys were two such famous toreutists.

The brilliant work of A. Riegl (*Spätrömische Kunstindustrie*, published in 1901), which was chiefly concerned with the minor arts of a period that had hitherto been considered decadent and unworthy of interest, was the source for a fundamental change of outlook in the study of Classical art. Laying stress, as he did, on the historical background of art and introducing the concept of *Kunstwollen*, the 'will to artistic production', Riegl judged a work of art no longer simply by reference to an ideal standard (which had been, generally speaking, Greek art of the 5th and 4th centuries BC) but in terms of a particular artistic vision or taste of which each object was the expression and the product. His book had the effect both of re-evaluating periods in the history of art which had been despised or ignored and of bringing into greater prominence the minor arts which, in the last analysis, are just as important as expressions of a historical period and just as vital to understanding it as the major arts. We shall see, in fact, that in certain periods and among certain peoples the minor or applied arts are quite purely and simply major art; this is true of the nomadic peoples of central Asia among whom there never was, nor could have been, any architecture or sculpture. It is true, too, of the late Roman and early Medieval periods when little by little the art of major sculpture ceased to exist. According to the old-fashioned view this was proof merely of artistic decadence, but according to Riegl it demonstrated the change from the plastic or tactile art of the Classical world to the new 'optical' taste typical of the Medieval world.

This new approach, however, creates a difficulty in preparing a history of jewellery; in some periods, for example the Greek 'Orientalising' period or the 'late antique', jewellery has a real value in the history of art, whereas in others it is reduced to a minor craft, as it was in Classical Greece or the Roman republic. Behind the various changes of taste there are always economic and social factors to be taken into account; the art of the goldsmith is one which can only flourish in periods of economic prosperity, and especially when there is an aristocratic social structure. In the case of republican Rome the attitude of the patrician families and their traditional opposition to any form of luxury was a powerful influence; one has only to think of the various sumptuary laws (against ostentation) which were brought in, generally with very little success, right up to the time of the late Roman Empire.

The difficulty, or rather the impossibility, of

providing a systematic history of a subject-matter so variable and elusive, explains why it is only in recent years that books have begun to appear specifically devoted to ancient jewellery. Other difficulties are the lack of fundamental publications, such as museum catalogues, and the problem of dating the various examples. The repetition of popular types is particularly marked in the case of jewellery where the same designs go on being made for centuries; moreover jewellery is handed down from generation to generation so that even if it is found in a tomb together with dated objects we cannot be sure that it is not considerably earlier than the rest. To identify the different centres of manufacture is another, almost insurmountable, problem because jewellery passed very easily from one place to another. Controversy rages over the place of manufacture of many examples of archaic jewellery from Italy; the necklace from Ruvo in the Museo Nazionale at Naples is variously assigned to workshops in Etruria and Magna Graecia.

However, despite these difficulties, our knowledge is certainly far better than it was a few years ago, thanks to a number of recent general studies and detailed researches. The increasing interest in jewellery is proved by the number of recent exhibitions devoted to the subject. One exhibition of treasures from the museums of Taranto and the Villa Giulia and Terme museums in Rome was held at the Palazzo Venezia in Rome in 1946; another was held at Bologna

1   Seven rectangular gold plaques. From Rhodes. 7th century
BC. British Museum, London.

2　Rectangular gold plaque. From Camirus. 7th century BC.
British Museum, London.

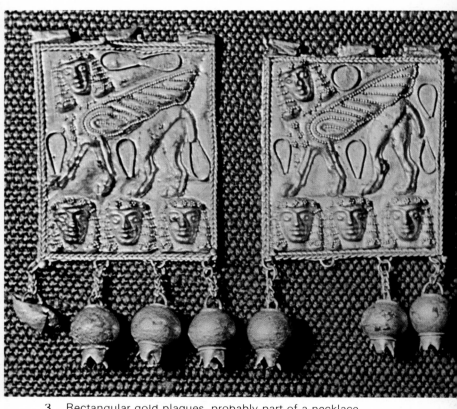

3 Rectangular gold plaques, probably part of a necklace.
From Camirus. 7th century BC. British Museum, London.

1 Seven rectangular gold plaques. From Rhodes. 7th century BC. British Museum, London. The plaques belong to a necklace. Each one has a figure of the Oriental Artemis or 'Mistress of the Animals' in repoussé relief; she is shown frontal, winged and dressed in a stiff mantle, with a lion rampant on either side of her. Rhodian Orientalising style.

2 Rectangular gold plaque. From Camirus. 7th century BC. British Museum, London. The row of beading along three sides is stamped out; the figure of the Oriental Artemis with her heavy face and Persian headdress is in repoussé relief. Rhodian Orientalising style.

3 Rectangular gold plaques, probably part of a necklace. From Camirus. 7th century BC. British Museum, London. The repoussé relief shows a sphinx in profile to the left with its head turned frontal; below are three female heads. Details are picked out by means of granulation. Rhodian Orientalising style.

4 Gold cup. From Sicily. 7th century BC. British Museum, London. The relief decoration consists of a slow, stately procession of six bulls. Siculo-Greek work.

4   Gold cup. From Sicily. 7th century BC. British Museum,
London.

in 1958, dealing with gold and silver from ancient Emilia and a very important one at Turin in 1961 (*Ori e argenti dell'Italia Antica*).

This brief account is concerned with Greek and Roman jewellery, including Etruscan jewellery, which is so closely related to it. It begins with the geometric period in Greece and excludes the Minoan and Mycenean periods; both of these, the former especially, are better treated in connection with the great Bronze Age civilisations of the Near East rather than with the later Greek world from which they are separated by a clear-cut historical division. The book ends with the period which marks the end of the Classical world and the beginning of the Medieval, the period generally called 'late antique'. Within these limits there is a relatively uniform development which establishes a consistent artistic tradition that can be followed from the 9th century BC to the age of Constantine.

The Geometric and Orientalising Periods in Greece and Etruria

The Greeks rightly connected the origins of jewellery with Eastern civilisations. The discovery was attributed to a mythical people, the Telchines, and frightening legends connected with mining and trading of gold with the Arimaspians, one-eyed men who fought perpetually with the griffins who guarded the precious metal. These mines are generally thought to be in central Asia, probably in the Altai region. A Greek poet, Aristeas of Proconnesus, who flourished probably in the 7th century BC, wrote a poem based on these legends.

The art of the goldsmith, which is essentially a courtly art, was introduced into Greece from the Oriental world, from Egypt and Mesopotamia. Phoenician trade must have played an important part in this; the importance of the Phoenicians as intermediaries is clear from Homer. However, for most of the first half of the 1st millennium BC, the mainland of Greece was poor in precious metalwork, and this is certainly to be explained by the comparative economic poverty of the Greek city-states in this period. It is only in the 8th century BC, towards the end of the geometric period, that gold objects begin to be found in tombs; the most important discoveries of this period have been made at Athens, Eleusis and Eretria. The commonest objects are pieces of gold sheet with figured reliefs inspired by oriental motifs, though still basically in the geometric style. Originally these sheets were used to decorate wooden boxes containing the ashes of the dead. Their funerary purpose is, therefore, quite clear, and the importance of funerary practices in Athens during this period is shown by the magnificent geometric vases of 'Dipylon' style which were placed above the tombs and are often of monumental scale. A passage of Homer where he describes the funerary rites of Hector throws light on the decorated cinerary urns (Homer, *Iliad* XXIV, 790 ff.); 'But when the daughter of Dawn, rosy-fingered Morning, shone forth, then gathered the folk around glorious Hector's pyre. First quenched they with bright wine all the burning, so far as the fire's strength went, and then his brethren and comrades gathered his white bones lamenting, and big tears flowed down their cheeks. And the bones they took and laid in a golden urn, shrouding them with soft purple robes, and straightway laid the urn in a hollow grave . . .'

Besides Attica, where some very fine craftsmanship

5   Gold fibula with serpentine bow. From Marsiliana d'Albegna. Second half of the 7th century BC. Museo Archeologico, Florence.

was carried out even in this early period, there were centres in Corinth, Crete and the islands of the Aegean in general. These were the areas where during the 'Orientalising' period, from the beginning of the 7th century BC onwards, the art of jewellery was rapidly developed. In Crete the most important finds are those of the Idaean Cave and a tomb at Cnossus, both of which contain some clearly imported objects of Syro-Phoenician manufacture, influenced by the art of Egypt and of Assyria. Similar influences can also be seen in the locally produced jewellery. In the islands and the coast of Asia Minor, a highly developed

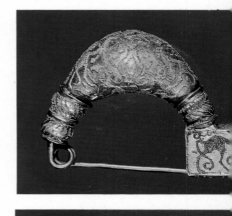

6 Gold 'leech' fibula. From the Tomb of the Lictor, Vetulonia. Second half of the 7th century BC. Museo Archeologico, Florence.

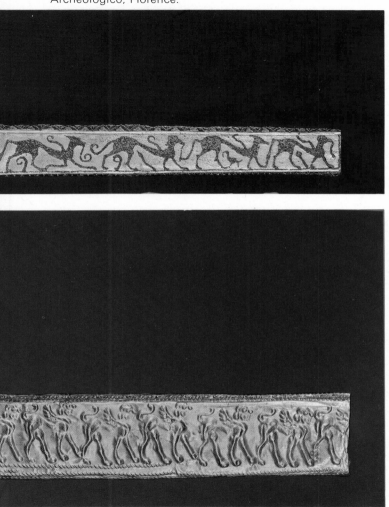

7 Gold 'leech' fibula. From the Tomb of the Lictor, Vetulonia. Second half of the 7th century BC. Museo Archeologico, Florence.

5   Gold fibula with serpentine bow. From Marsiliana d'Albegna. Second half of the 7th century BC. Museo Archeologico, Florence. Little figures of ducklings are soldered on the catch-plate and the bow; these were stamped out and decorated with granulation. The fibula is also decorated with granulated patterns of zigzags and maeander. North Etruscan Orientalising style.

6   Gold 'leech' fibula. From the Tomb of the Lictor, Vetulonia. Second half of the 7th century BC. Museo Archeologico, Florence. The long catch-plate is decorated on both sides with a procession of five animals, carried out in extremely fine granulation. On one side the animals move to the right, on the other, to the left. North Etruscan Orientalising style.

7 Gold 'leech' fibula. From the Tomb of the Lictor, Vetulonia. Second half of the 7th century BC. Museo Archeologico, Florence. The long catch-plate is decorated with a line of winged sphinxes moving to the right, worked in repoussé relief. The relief is framed by a rope pattern; on the upper surface are a series of Phoenician palmettes. North Etruscan Orientalising style.

8 Gold fibula with serpentine bow. From Vulci. 7th century BC. British Museum, London. A series of little lions is soldered on to the fibula; these were stamped out and the detail added by granulation. Granulation was also used for the geometric patterns on the bow. South Etruscan work.

8 Gold fibula with serpentine bow. From Vulci. 7th century BC. British Museum, London.

and cosmopolitan society was now being created; the cities of Miletus, Ephesus, Smyrna, Tralles, Camirus on Rhodes, and the island of Cyprus, where Greek and Oriental influences met and mingled, now enjoyed a remarkable prosperity deriving from their favoured positions for trade between East and West.

Rhodes, especially the cemetery of Camirus, has yielded a considerable number of gold objects; one of the commonest types is the rectangular pendant with representations of the Mistress of the Animals, of Melissa, the anthropomorphic bee, or of a sphinx. There are some particularly fine examples in the British Museum, London; the very high technical skill, which is characteristic of all the Ionian jewellery, is combined with a clear understanding of the possibilities of the material. Plain surfaces, worked in relief with a keen sense of form, are combined with minute detailing in granulation and filigree. The jewellery from Ephesus, most of it from the votive deposit in the Sanctuary of Artemis, has its own characteristics; granulation is almost entirely absent and simple, delicate motifs predominate. There were about six hundred of these objects, mainly of the 7th century BC, and they include fibulae (brooches), earrings, pins with ovoid heads, and figurines made of stamped gold sheet.

Another very important centre from the middle of the 7th century BC was Cyprus, which must have been one of the chief markets of precious metals in the Mediterranean. A composite style developed out of the different ethnic and cultural influences – Greek, Syro-Palestinian and Egyptian; in jewellery the Oriental taste for richness and luxury is clear and offers a close comparison with contemporary Etruscan work.

Altogether the most interesting examples of Orientalising jewellery come from the Greek islands and Ionia. The elaborate figured designs, especially in Rhodian work, are particularly notable. The techniques of filigree and granulation, which had been invented a long time before in the Eastern world, achieved in this period an unrivalled perfection. The typically Oriental taste for elaboration of ornament is balanced by the Greek feeling for organic structure which is so apparent in their art from geometric times onwards. In the first half of the 7th century BC, jewellery, together with pottery and small bronzework, was a very important branch of art, the most acceptable to a society which was basically aristocratic and whose prosperity was increasingly founded upon commerce.

The unexpected development of an Orientalising civilisation in 7th-century Etruria, following on a period of comparative poverty known as the Villanovan, has often been connected with the mythical account of the immigration of the Etruscans from the Eastern world, from Lydia according to Herodotus.

Nowadays, the idea of a large-scale invasion in such a late period is generally, and rightly, rejected, and the phenomenon is explained more logically by the development of trade and commerce between East and West, by Greek colonisation in southern Italy from the middle of the 8th century and, especially, by the appearance of Phocaeo-Ionian influence in the Tyrrhenian area. One of the main reasons for the sudden interest in Etruria was the exploitation of the iron mines of Elba. Etruscan metallurgy soon became famous; the most important centre was Populonia in whose neighbourhood have been found vast deposits of iron slag accumulated over many centuries. The immigration into Etruria of groups of artists from mainland Greece, the islands and Asia Minor is highly probable and is confirmed by the testimony of ancient writers. Pliny, for example, records the arrival at Tarquinia of a certain Demaratus, a Corinthian, who was accompanied by artists with the significant names of Eucheir, Diopos and Eugrammos.

One can, however, be certain that most of the Orientalising objects found in Etruria were made locally. An early phase, when manufactured objects were imported, was followed by a second in which artists from the eastern Mediterranean founded local workshops which soon developed a distinctive local style. The chief workshops must have been situated in the commercial cities which were generally near the sea; they not only acquired economic and political importance but also became genuine cultural centres. As far as jewellery is concerned Vetulonia in northern Etruria and Caere in the south were probably the chief centres of manufacture.

At Vetulonia the commonest objects are the leech-fibulae with long catch-plate, spherical-headed pins, bracelets and earrings. The decoration is chiefly carried out by granulation, a technique which achieves an unrivalled perfection in this period; the grains of gold are sometimes so small that they look like gold-dust. Whereas in south Etruscan jewellery granulation is used only for the details of figures modelled in relief, in the north granulation is made to produce complete silhouettes rather like the glaze on Athenian black-figure vases. The result is perhaps more refined and elegant but certainly more monotonous than the products of Caere and Praeneste in the south. It is in these latter places and in Faliscan territory that we find the most characteristic examples of Etruscan Orientalising art.

It was at Caere, certainly one of the great centres of the Mediterranean world, that Etruscan Orientalising civilisation was first recognised by scholars, long before excavation in Greece and the East had provided the evidence for a correct interpretation of it. In 1836 the dean Regolini and General Galassi looked with astonished eyes on the grave of a princely Etruscan family with its immensely rich contents of bronze, silver and gold which are now the chief

9 Gold pendant. From the Regolini-Galassi tomb, Caere.
7th century BC. Museo Gregoriano, Vatican.

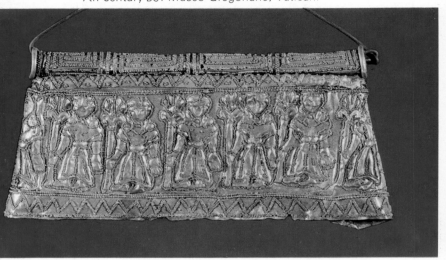

10 Pectoral of gold sheet. From the Regolini-Galassi tomb, Caere. 7th century BC. Museo Gregoriano, Vatican.

9   Gold pendant. From the Regolini-Galassi tomb, Caere. 7th century BC Museo Gregoriano, Vatican. A sheet of gold, trapezoidal in shape, is joined to a gold tube decorated with granulated maeander pattern; the sheet has a series of female figures in relief, each holding a fan. South Etruscan Orientalising style.

10   Pectoral of gold sheet. From the Regolini-Galassi tomb, Caere. 7th century BC. Museo Gregoriano, Vatican. The gold sheet was once fixed to a bronze backing which is now lost. The decorative motifs include semicircles, columns, volutes, winged lions, deer, female figures, chimaeras and rampant lions. South Etruscan Orientalising style.

11   Gold earring. From the Regolini-Galassi tomb. Caere. 7th century BC. Museo Gregoriano, Vatican. The decoration was stamped, with granulate details; the design is very like that of the gold pendant (plate 9) from the same tomb. South Etruscan Orientalising style.

12   Large gold fibula. From the Regolini-Galassi tomb, Caere. 7th century BC. Museo Gregoriano, Vatican. The disc is decorated with five lions, framed by a double border of interlacing arches with rosettes. On the bow are little figures of lions and cocks, stamped and granulated. South Etruscan Orientalising style.

11   Gold earring. From the Regolini-Galassi tomb, Caere.
7th century BC. Museo Gregoriano, Vatican.

12 Large gold fibula. From the Regolini-Galassi tomb, Caere. 7th century BC. Museo Gregoriano, Vatican.

treasure of the Museo Gregoriano Etrusco in the Vatican. These objects remained unique only for a few decades, until excavation at Palestrina brought to light two rich Orientalising tombs, the Barberini Tomb (now in the Villa Guilia Museum, Rome) and the Bernardini Tomb (now in the Museo Pigorini, Rome).

This remarkable early Etruscan jewellery provides abundant proof of the high economic and artistic level reached by the southern Etruscans in the 7th century BC. The contents of the Regolini-Galassi tomb include a gold pectoral decorated with parallel bands of reliefs, an enormous gold fibula (over a foot long) with complicated ornament, various pendants, some earrings and a necklace with three large pendants containing pieces of amber. A careful study of the fibula shows the mastery of these artists in a number of different techniques. The elliptical bow of the fibula is decorated with little figures of ducks in the round, made of stamped gold sheets soldered together; these are arranged in seven rows, and the spaces between them are filled by winged lions in repoussé relief with granulated details. Above this there are two little parallel bars with zigzag pattern in granulation, and on the elliptical disc, which is framed by a border of interlacing arches with rosettes, there are five lions, symmetrically arranged, worked in repoussé; the outlines and the manes are added in granulation. The effect is a clever contrast between areas of crowded decoration and areas in which the figures are spread out on plain surfaces; there is a remarkable understanding of the possibilities of the material which allows both smooth shining surfaces and the most minutely detailed granulation, as well as various intermediate effects. In the earrings and pendants one finds the use of repoussé to produce the low relief figures, while lines of granulation define and pick out the convex surfaces. The result is extremely effective and contrasts with the jewellery of northern Etruria where granulation is used to cover large surfaces producing two-dimensional, linear effects.

The jewellery found in the cemetery of Praeneste during the second half of the last century is of the same high quality as the Caeretan. The big rectangular plaque from the Bernardini Tomb is richly decorated with various fantastic animals – chimaeras, winged felines, sphinxes – modelled in the round and very like those of the Regolini-Galassi fibula. The other gold objects, fibulae, pins etc., are all of similar style and prove the existence of a local school of craftsmen of the highest ability, closely connected with the other centres of southern Etruria. It seems likely, to judge from the close similarity between the Caeretan and Praenestine jewellery that the best pieces are the work of immigrant Etruscan artists; Etruscans were certainly present in Praeneste at this time as they were in Rome. Soon local schools will have developed; there is plenty of evidence for this including the famous 'Praeneste fibula' now in the Pigorini Museum at Rome which has the signature of its maker written in archaic Latin: 'MANIOS MED VHEVHAKED NUMASIOI' ('Manios made me for Numerios'). Pliny too (*Naturalis Historia* xxxiii, 61) mentions the skill of the Praenestine goldsmiths.

The quality of this Orientalising Etruscan jewellery is still far from being truly appreciated. A proper estimate of its quality has been hampered by a rigidly 'Classicising' point of view. Expressions like 'overloaded ornament', 'provincialism' and 'barbarism' crop up again and again, and little account is taken of the fact that jewellery by its very nature and the character of the materials it uses – gold, stones and enamels – achieves its fullest expression in those civilisations and among those peoples who are furthest removed from Classical ideals of harmony and balance. The jewellery of Classical Greece is far less impressive than that of the Orientalising or Hellenistic periods, and in Etruria during the 7th century BC we have one of the best and most convincing expressions of the essential character of jewellery of any period.

Archaic Greece and Etruria
The archaic period in Greece is very badly documented; our knowledge is derived chiefly from written sources, from pictures on painted pottery and from examples of jewellery which come generally from the

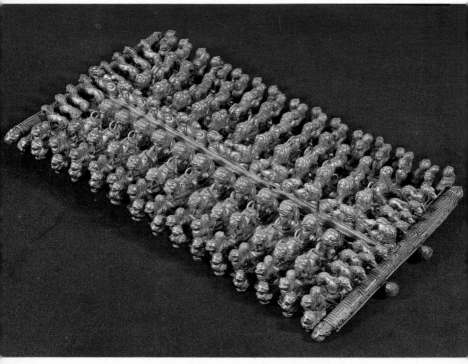

13 Rectangular gold plaque. From the Bernardini Tomb, Praeneste. 7th century BC. Pigorini Museum, Rome.

14 Gold bracelet. From Praeneste. 7th century BC. Once in the Castellani Collection, now in the British Museum, London.

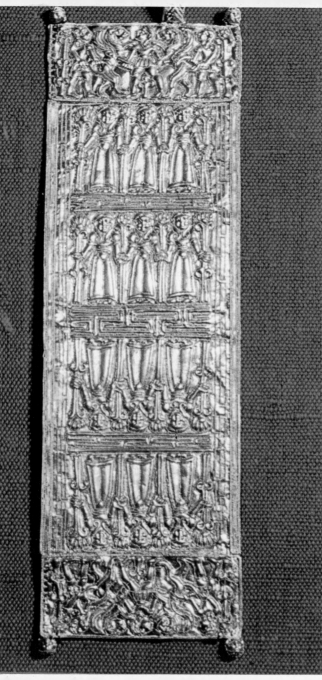

13 Rectangular gold plaque. From the Bernardini Tomb, Praeneste. 7th century BC. Pigorini Museum, Rome. The decoration consists of real and fantastic animals, including lions, horses, harpies and chimaeras with human heads on their backs; the figures were stamped out and the details added with granulation. South Etruscan Orientalising style.

14 Gold bracelet. From Praeneste. 7th century BC. Once in the Castellani Collection, now in the British Museum, London. The decoration, in repoussé with granulation, is arranged in bands; the main decorative motif is once again the rows of female figures holding fans. South Etruscan Orientalising style.

15 Gold buckle of comb-like shape. From the Bernardini Tomb, Praeneste. 7th century BC. Pigorini Museum, Rome. Gold rods, looking like the teeth of a comb, are soldered on one side. The flat part is decorated with stamped reliefs; these are flying birds, two human-headed lions heraldically placed in the centre, and two running lions at the ends. The border and the details of the figures are granulated. South Etruscan Orientalising style.

16 Rectangular gold plaque. From the Barberini Tomb, Praeneste. 7th century BC. Villa Giulia Museum, Rome. The decoration consists of various fantastic animals, including winged felines, sphinxes and chimaeras. At the corners there are four feline heads on long curving necks. South Etruscan Orientalising style.

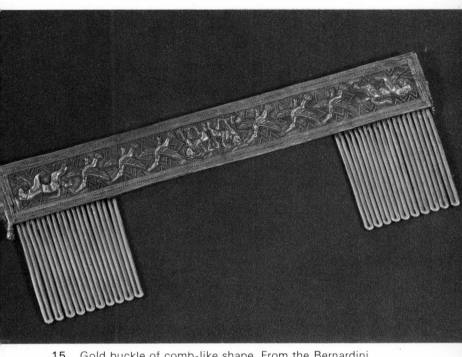

15 Gold buckle of comb-like shape. From the Bernardini
Tomb, Praeneste. 7th century BC. Pigorini Museum, Rome.

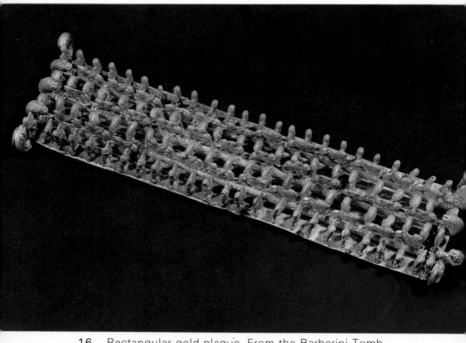

16 Rectangular gold plaque. From the Barberini Tomb,
Praeneste. 7th century BC. Villa Giulia Museum, Rome.

peripheral regions of the Greek world. Oriental influence still predominates. The wealth of several more or less Hellenised rulers of Asia Minor was proverbial in Greece. One thinks particularly of the mythical Midas, King of Phrygia, and later, in the 6th century BC, of Croesus of Lydia. Herodotus and other ancient writers have a number of references to the Lydian king's offerings at the chief sanctuaries of Greece; the gold tripods in the sanctuary of Apollo Ismenius in Boeotia, the gold shield in the temple of Athena Pronaia, the offerings in the Ionian sanctuaries, especially the Didymaion at Miletus and the Artemision of Ephesus. For the reconstruction of the Artemision Croesus gave a series of columns, with sculptured reliefs on the lower part, and gold statues of oxen. Fine jewellery from Lydia is mentioned by the lyric poets between the end of the 7th century BC and the beginning of the 6th. Alcman mentions the typical Lydian diadem, the *mitra*, and Sappho, in a recently discovered ode, consoles her daughter Cleis to whom she cannot give one because Pittacus, the tyrant of Mytilene, had introduced legislation against excessive luxury. Similar laws were introduced almost everywhere in Greece and the colonies, a phenomenon which is connected with the breakdown of aristocratic rule and the establishment of tyrannies in the Greek world.

These developments explain the reduction in the output of jewellery in the 6th century BC. The types, too, become simpler and more severe. In sharp contrast, the Homeric *Hymn to Aphrodite*, of 7th century date, describes the goddess in all the richness of her adornment:

> 'She wore a dress brighter than the flames of fire,
> Spiral bracelets, gleaming flower-earrings and
> Beautiful necklaces on her delicate neck,
> All of gold, superbly wrought.'

At this time men, too, wore jewellery. The custom of adorning the hair with golden cicades was widespread, and rings were very common. If private luxury diminished in the 6th century BC, the custom of offering jewels and gold to the gods increased rapidly, as did the use of precious materials for statuary, especially the chryselephantine technique with ivory for the flesh parts and gold for the drapery. Among the objects of this period which are described to us in detail by ancient authors is the chest which Cypselus, tyrant of Corinth and father of Periander, offered to the sanctuary of Olympia. It was made of cedar-wood with gold and ivory veneer. Cypselus also dedicated, again at Olympia, a gold statue of Zeus.

The enormous regard for gold, characteristic of aristocratic society, continued through the whole archaic period, and we find echoes of it still in the early 5th century when Pindar writes (*Olympian* 1, 1 ff.): 'Water is best of all things, but gold shines like fire in the night, above all great riches'; or again:

'Gold is Zeus's child. Nothing corrodes nor consumes it. It conquers the mind of men, and is the most powerful of possessions'.

Outside mainland Greece there were different developments. When Ionia was conquered by the Persians, the links between the Asiatic Greeks and the Oriental world became more direct. The exchange of ideas between the Greek and Iranian worlds became more intense until it reached its climax after Alexander the Great in the Hellenistic period. Herodotus several times recalls the enormous impression which the Persian wealth in precious metals made upon the Greeks. His description (Book ix, 80, Rawlinson's translation) of the booty taken by the Greeks after Plataea is typical:

'Then Pausanias made a proclamation that no one should touch the booty, but that the Helots should collect it and bring it to one place. So the Helots went and spread themselves through the camp, wherein they found many tents richly adorned with furniture of gold and silver, many couches covered with plates of the same, and many golden bowls, goblets and other drinking vessels. On the carriages were bags containing silver and golden cauldrons; and the bodies of the slain furnished bracelets and chains, and scimitars with golden ornaments – not to mention embroidered apparel, of which no one made any account. The Helots at this time stole many things of much value, which they sold in after times to the

17 Gold buckle. From the Barberini Tomb, Praeneste. 7th century BC. Villa Giulia Museum, Rome.

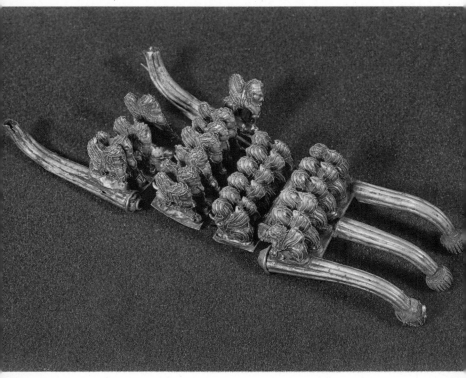

18   Gold cup. From Praeneste. 7th century BC. Victoria and
Albert Museum, London.

17   Gold buckle. From the Barberini Tomb. Praeneste. 7th century BC. Villa Giulia Museum, Rome. The buckle is made up of two parts, joined by little rings; the decoration consists of four parallel rows of winged felines and chimaeras. South Etruscan Orientalising style.

18   Gold cup. From Praeneste. 7th century BC. Victoria and Albert Museum, London. The tall cylindrical neck is decorated with two bands of maeander ornament and a band of double interlace pattern. The body of the cup has a series of convex ribs narrowing towards the bottom; between the ribs is a granulated herring-bone pattern. South Etruscan Orientalising style.

19   Gold bracelets or earrings. From Vetulonia. 7th century BC. Museo Archeologico, Florence. Plain bands alternate with openwork filigree bands; at each end are three female heads wearing volute curls. North Etruscan Orientalising style.

20   Gold fibula with serpentine bow. From Praeneste. End of the 7th century BC. Pigorini Museum, Rome. On the bow are two large spheres and four buttons. On the catch-plate there is an inscription in archaic Latin: MANIOS MED VHEVHAKED NUMASIOI ('Manios made me for Numerios').

19 Gold bracelets or earrings. From Vetulonia. 7th century
BC. Museo Archeologico, Florence.

20 Gold fibula with serpentine bow. From Praeneste. End of the 7th century BC. Pigorini Museum, Rome.

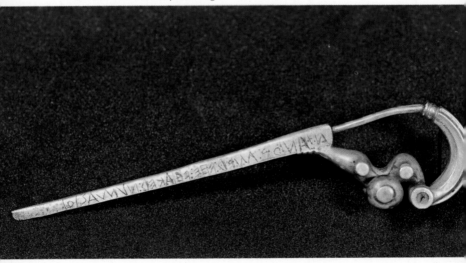

Aeginetans; however, they brought in likewise no small quantity, chiefly such things as it was not possible for them to hide. And this was the beginning of the great wealth of the Aeginetans, who bought the gold of the Helots as if it were mere brass.'

Then he describes (Book ix, 81) the use to which this vast treasure was put:

'When all the booty had been brought together, a tenth of the whole was set apart for the Delphian god; and hence was made the golden tripod which stands on the bronze serpent with the three heads, quite close to the altar. Portions were also set apart for the gods of Olympia and of the Isthmus, from which were made, in the one case, a bronze Jupiter ten cubits high, and, in the other, a bronze Neptune of seven cubits. After this, the rest of the spoil was divided among the soldiers, each of whom received less or more according to his deserts; and in this way a distribution was made of the Persian concubines, of the gold, the silver, the beasts of burthen, and all the other valuables.'

The 6th century BC was the period of Ionian greatness. Ionian influence was felt not only in Athens but in Doric cities such as Syracuse where, towards the end of the century the Temple of Athena was reconstructed in Ionic style. The *korai* (statues of young women) of the Acropolis at Athens wear some types of jewellery which are certainly of Ionian origin, among them the disc earrings. Among other forms of earrings which come in during this period are one with a pendant in the form of an inverted pyramid, which continues in use down to the late Hellenistic period, and one in the form of a bunch of grapes. The diadem of sheet gold, decorated with stamped reliefs, survives from the earlier period.

The most notable discoveries of jewellery, as we have seen, have been made outside the boundaries of mainland Greece – in the Greco-Scythian, Greco-Thracian, Greco-Etruscan and Greco-Celtic areas. All this jewellery shows a common Ionian influence, but now the differences between the various centres are less marked than they were before, so that we can speak of a true *koine* (common language), the predecessor of the Attic *koine* in the next century.

Greco-Scythian jewellery arises from the connections between the Greek cities of the north coast of the Black Sea, in southern Russia, and the Scythian peoples. In the 6th century BC there began a large output which continued right through the Hellenistic period, and the jewellery forms one of the chief glories of the Hermitage Museum in Leningrad. The most striking discoveries are those of the royal tumulus burials in the Kuban. The mixture of styles and subject-matter is extremely interesting. The subjects, hunting, fantastic beasts, are generally to the taste of the person who ordered the jewellery, but the style has an Iranian element, overlaid with Ionian Greek influence. The immense richness of these discoveries must be explained by the artistic needs of a nomadic or semi-nomadic people, by the aristocratic structure of Scythian society, and especially by the local funerary customs which are described in detail by Herodotus (Book iv, ii, 71):

'Then the body of the dead king is laid in the grave prepared for it, stretched upon a mattress; spears are fixed in the ground on either side of the corpse . . . In the open space around the body of the king they bury one of his concubines, first killing her by strangling, and also his cupbearer, his cook, his groom, his lacquey, his messenger, some of his horses, firstlings of all his other possessions, and some golden cups; for they use neither silver nor brass. After this they set to work and raise a vast mound above the grave, all of them vying with each other and seeking to make it as tall as possible.'

In Italy the output of jewellery continues, especially in Magna Graecia and Etruria. The products of these two areas were becoming more and more like one another under the common influence of Ionian Greece. In many cases it is difficult to distinguish one from the other, and the attributions of particular pieces to the different schools are usually highly controversial. In southern Italy Ruvo has been the richest source of jewellery, though nothing has been found at Taranto which was later to become the chief centre of production in Italy. The outstanding discovery is the necklace with pendants found at Ruvo, now in the National Museum at Naples (plate

21 Pendant made of gold sheet. From Noicattaro. 6th century BC. Museo Archeologico, Bari.

22   Gold ring. From S. Angelo Muxaro. Late 6th — early 5th
century BC. Museo Archeologico Nazionale, Syracuse.

21   Pendant made of gold sheet. From Noicattaro. 6th century BC. Museo Archeologico, Bari. The principal motif is a running hare framed by ornamental borders of rosettes and guilloche; the decoration is in repoussé. Below are three little pendants in the form of lotus buds. Archaic south Italian.

22   Gold ring. From S. Angelo Muxaro. Late 6th – early 5th century BC. Museo Archeologico Nazionale, Syracuse. The bezel has an intaglio figure of a wolf with its tongue hanging out and its tail curled upwards. The bezel served as a seal. Siculo-Greek work.

23   Gold necklace. From Ruvo. 6th century BC Museo Archeologico Nazionale, Taranto. The necklace is composed of a series of ribbed biconical beads and pendants in the form of female heads with long tresses. Archaic south Italian.

24   Gold necklace. From Ruvo. End of 6th – early 5th century BC. Museo Archeologico Nazionale, Naples. The necklace consists of interlaced gold wire forming a network linked with a series of pendants of various forms – lotus flowers, acorns and Silenus heads. Archaic south Italian or Etruscan.

23 Gold necklace. From Ruvo. 6th century BC. Museo
Archeologico Nazionale, Taranto.

24   Gold necklace. From Ruvo. End of 6th – early 5th
century BC. Museo Archeologico Nazionale, Naples.

24). It consists of a band of interlaced gold with a net hanging from it, to which various pendants are attached – acorns, lotus flowers, Silenus heads. The technique is exquisite; one notes especially the method of indicating the rough surface of the acorn cup with minute granulation, while the acorn itself is worked in smooth sheet. The Silenus heads are superbly detailed, with granulation for the hair and finely chased detail on the beards. Despite this close attention to detail, the overall design loses nothing; there is a skilful alternation of void and solid, and the various motifs are designed to complement one another. Breglia thought that the necklace was Etruscan, but it may be that we should look for its place of manufacture in Campania where the Greek and Etruscan element lived side by side for a long time. Also from Ruvo is another necklace, earlier in date (perhaps of the early 6th century BC) and now in the Taranto museum. It is composed of a series of beads of lens-shape, alternating with female heads in relief. The heads with their long oval eyes, the beaded hair style and the typical archaic smile are clearly archaic Ionian in style.

Another form invented at this time is the ring with elongated, eye-shaped bezel which began to supersede the older type of ring, Egyptian in origin, with swivelling scarab. There are a number of fine examples of the new type, decorated with figures of animals, in the National Museum at Syracuse. Later the bezel becomes broader until it develops into the oval form characteristic of the Classical and Hellenistic periods.

One might, but with considerable caution, attribute to a south Italian workshop the famous diadem of Vix found north of Dijon in 1953 together with the massive bronze *crater* (64½ in high) decorated with military scenes which was almost certainly made in Magna Graecia. The diadem, in dimensions and weight (16 oz.), is a unique piece, and this makes its dating and attribution all the more difficult. It consists of a gold tube curved in an arc of a circle narrowing slightly at the ends and terminating in feline claws with large spherical finials soldered to them. At the junction are little figures of Pegasus, made of solid gold, which rest on little round bases decorated with filigree. The piece is remarkable for its simplicity and for its keen sense of form and volume, and the decoration is all the more effective for being confined to two places. The diadem belongs to the turn of the 6th and 5th centuries when the florid ornamental Ionic style was giving way to more restrained forms; the Classical period is near.

In Etruria there was, as we have seen a strong Ionian Greek influence, as, indeed, there was in every branch of Etruscan art, especially painting. In distinguishing the different phases of Etruscan culture this is usually called the period of Ionian influence, though other influences may be detected, including that of Athens. The large scale importation of Athenian pottery now begins, black-figure at first and later red-figure, superseding the products of Corinthian workshops. The role of Athens in the Etruscan artistic tradition increases steadily until it becomes completely dominant at the end of the 5th century.

In Etruria, too, the scarab-ring disappears in the course of the 6th century BC and is replaced by the type with elongated oval bezel; at first the bezel is divided into two zones but later has a single field. The earliest motifs, which are incised, still belong to the Orientalising tradition, but Greek mythological subjects are soon introduced. The similarity between these Etruscan rings and the products of goldsmiths in Asia Minor is so clear that they must have been the work of Ionian artists. However, even here it is very difficult to distinguish the work of Ionian goldsmiths from that of Etruscan goldsmiths working in Ionian style. Another fairly widespread form of jewellery is the necklace with gold pendants similar to the example from Ruvo (plate 24) which has already been described. One such necklace from a site somewhere in the Etruscan Maremma, is now in the British Museum. Another novelty is the basket-type earring which is certainly of Etruscan origin; its use spread in the 6th century BC, and it continued to be made throughout the 5th. In these objects which are certainly local we can follow the different tendencies in Etruscan craftsmanship during the archaic period. Granulation becomes less skilful and gives way to filigree; stamped details, in high relief, are popular and are sometimes cut out and arranged to imitate flowers and leaves. In figured work the granulation is used only for the background, a complete inversion of the technique found in the Vetulonia jewellery of the Orientalising period; the change is not unlike that which took place in Athenian pottery when the technique of painting black figures on the natural clay colour of the vase gave way to red-figure where the background is painted in black and the figures stand out in the natural colour of the clay. The change in jewellery as well as pottery made it possible to add refinements to the internal detail of the figures which were not, as before, mere silhouettes.

Of particular interest are some little figures of women in Ionic costume, made of repoussé gold, sometimes with details added in glass paste. Style and iconography link these figures with Ionian art, but the taste for colour and elaborate ornament is typical of the south Etruscan orbit in which they were produced (Caere or Vulci). Here, as elsewhere, we note a tendency to polychromy, with the use of coloured stones or glass inserted, for example, into the pendants of necklaces. The exclusive use of gold had been characteristic of the Orientalising period. The inevitable result of this new tendency is a greater simplicity in the technique of working the gold; variety was now achieved by the use of different

25   Gold necklace. From S. Filippo di Osimo. Last years of the 6th century BC. Museo Nazionale, Ancona. This fine necklace, an outstanding piece, consists of 29 spheroid beads with two rams' heads, one at each end; the rams heads were stamped. Etruscan work.

26   Gold dagger-case. 4th century BC. Metropolitan Museum, New York. The reliefs show scenes of battle between Greeks and Barbarians and fights between animals; there is a pair of winged lions, arranged heraldically, at one end. Greco-Scythian work.

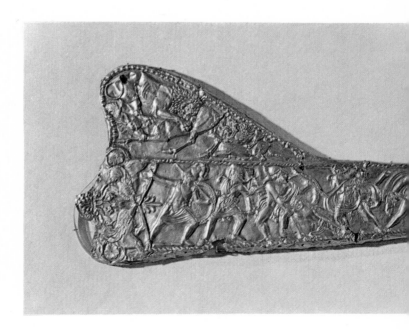

27 Gold pendant. Early 5th century BC. Victoria and Albert Museum, London. Probably a pendant from a necklace, in the form of a human head worked in repoussé relief. South Italian Greek work.

28 Gold Hercules' knot. From Ginosa. 4th century BC. Museo Archeologico Nazionale, Taranto. Perhaps the central part of a diadem. The knot is composed of interlacing bands; at either end there is a frieze with crenellated border, decorated with a rosette pattern. The surface of the knot is ornamented with filigree leaves and stems. Classical Greek work from Magna Graecia.

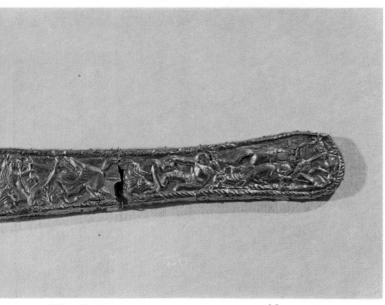

26 Gold dagger-case. 4th century BC. Metropolitan Museum, New York.

27 Gold pendant. Early 5th century BC. Victoria and Albert Museum, London.

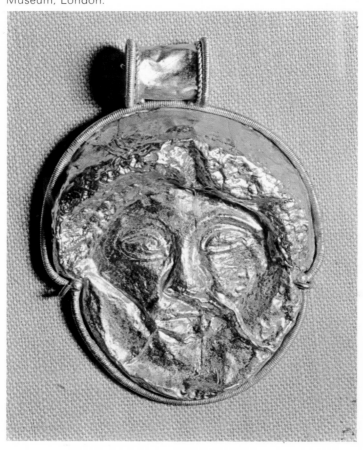

28 Gold Hercules knot. From Ginosa. 4th century BC. Museo Archeologico Nazionale, Taranto.

materials. As one scholar has justly observed, the use of gold is more and more confined to 'settings'; the process was now in its infancy but became more and more obvious in the course of the 5th century BC.

The Classical Period
The period which includes the end of the archaic and the beginning of the Classical age in Greece – broadly speaking the years between 500 and 450 BC – is very poorly documented by surviving jewellery. We can, however, build up some sort of picture on the basis of the literary sources, which were now more numerous and more precise, and from pictures on other monuments, especially Attic red-figure pottery. It is still the areas outside the Greek world proper – Thrace, southern Russia and Italy – which provide the chief evidence. Personal jewellery continued to be relatively modest and the work of the goldsmith was more and more devoted to offerings at the sanctuaries of the gods. We have surviving inventories of such offerings, including those of the Parthenon and of the temple treasure at Delos; the latter was compiled in 279 BC, but includes objects as early as the 4th century BC and even earlier. The inventory lists gold crowns, sacrificial dishes (1600 in all) and other vessels, rings, bracelets, pins, necklaces etc.

The work of the ablest artists was however devoted to the great projects of constructing the massive chryselephantine statues, especially after the middle of the 5th century BC. These were more than cult statues; they were gigantic offerings which, in fact, were looked upon as part of the state treasury. The statue of Athena Parthenos by Phidias was the chief nucleus of the treasury of the Delian League which had been transferred to Athens by Pericles from its original location in Delos. Pheidias' other statue, the Zeus of Olympia is known to us only from ancient descriptions; no faithful copy exists. Even less well known is the great chryselephantine statue of Hera made by Polykleitus for the sanctuary at Argos.

For the Zeus of Olympia we have a detailed description by Pausanias. The seated figure, about 40 feet high, was composed mainly of gold and ivory. Lucian tells us that a single lock of hair weighed nearly 6 lb. Other materials were used for small detail—ebony, precious stones, glass and obsidian. The recent excavations in Pheidias' workshop at Olympia yielded fragments of ivory, and clay moulds used to make the golden drapery of the god. There were also fragments of glass, obsidian and other stones serving to enrich various parts of the statue. It was, in effect, an enormous piece of goldsmith's work in which dozens of craftsmen must have taken part.

Turning to the Greco-Scythian sphere (this is chiefly southern Russia but, because of the close cultural connections, one may also include Thrace) we see that towards the end of the 5th century BC, and still more in the 4th, Greek influence increases.

Much of the jewellery must obviously be attributed to Greek craftsmen of the coastal cities (Olbia, Panticapaeum, Phanagoria) working to the orders of Scythians. The subject-matter reveals the culture of the patrons for this is chiefly taken from Scythian life, but the style is almost purely Greek. There is also a local production which carries on the earlier animal style.

Dating from the end of the 5th century BC is a splendid comb from the Solokha barrow, excavated in 1912-1913. The object is about 4 in long and decorated with a figured scene showing three warriors in combat, one on horseback. Their dress is Scythian and includes the characteristic trousers; the subject is, therefore, a battle between Barbarians. But if the subject is appropriate to the taste of the patron who was certainly a princely Scythian, the style is Greek. M. Rostovzev very plausibly attributed the work to Panticapaeum, the old capital of the Bosphoran kingdom. This very remarkable object should be dated in the last quarter of the 5th century; the style is post-Pheidian Greek. The use of necklaces with acorn pendants, like the ones on the necklace from Ruvo, continues in the 5th and 4th centuries BC, as we learn from a passage of Aristophanes (*Lysistrata*, line 407 f.) One example, which must be the work of Greek craftsmen, has been found at Nymphaeum in the Crimea. The influence of the post-Pheidian art of Athens, such as we have already seen in the Solokha comb, continues down to the end of the 4th century BC; good examples are the medallions from Kul-Oba, probably parts of earrings, which reproduce the head of the Athena Parthenos of Pheidias.

The jewellery of Thrace, and the closely related jewellery of Thessaly and Macedonia, also seems to be dependent on that of continental Greece in the 5th and 4th centuries BC. But the style, though purely Greek, is adapted to a local subject-matter. This is clear, for example, in some of the rings with oval bezel of the type that had originated in the late archaic period; here the figure of a horseman, a theme characteristic of every period of Thracian art, is frequently found. There are also more obviously provincial works where the influence of Scythian art is stronger.

The Treasure of Panagyurishte is one of the outstanding Thracian finds; it was discovered in a tumulus in 1949. The treasure consists of four *rhyta* or animal-head vases, three jugs, an amphora with the scene of Achilles on Scyros, and a circular dish with negro heads and acorns arranged concentrically. Here, too, we are concerned with the work of Greek artists of the second half of the 4th century BC commissioned by wealthy Thracians. Perhaps they were travelling artists who were prepared to work at a foreign court. The names of the persons involved in the scenes are inscribed, and the weight of each vessel is accurately given. The unit of measurement, which is Attic, and

29   Gold earring of 'leech' form. From Taranto. 4th century BC. Museo Archeologico Nazionale, Taranto. The bow is decorated with palmettes, scrolls and vine stems in filigree work. It is surmounted by a palmette flanked by scrolls and rosettes; at each end is a figure of Cupid. Chains hanging from the bow support little ornamental amphorae. Classical Greek work from Magna Graecia.

30   Pair of gold earrings. From Taranto. 4th century BC. Museo Archeologico Nazionale, Taranto. Curved tubes with rope-like twists ending at one end in a point and at the other in a lion's head. Classical Greek work from Magna Graecia.

31   Pair of gold earrings. From Taranto. Second half of the 4th century BC. Museo Archeologico Nazionale, Taranto. The body is formed of twisted gold wires; at the wider end there is a collar of filigree leaves, with the protoma of a lion issuing from it. A similar, but smaller, protoma forms the other end. Classical Greek work from south Italy.

Gold earring of 'leech' form. From Taranto. 4th century BC. Museo Archeologico Nazionale, Taranto.

30 Pair of gold earrings. From Taranto. 4th century BC Museo Archeologico Nazionale Taranto.

31 Pair of gold earrings. From Taranto. Second half of the 4th century BC. Museo Archeologico Nazionale Taranto.

the style suggest an attribution to some centre under Athenian influence rather than one in Asia Minor. The group as a whole is one of the most important that has survived from the Classical period.

In Magna Graecia from the end of the 5th century BC and especially in the 4th there is a vast increase in the production of jewellery; Etruria on the other hand was suffering a major economic and political crisis which is also apparent in art. The years after 400 BC were a flourishing period in Apulia. While the importation of Attic pottery decreased steadily, a local style was created under the inspiration of contemporary Attic pottery, especially the mannerist style of Meidias. Taranto became the most important centre in southern Italy, but Campania (Capua in particular) shared in this development and produced its own rich and varied pottery. The chief characteristic of this period is the remarkable homogeneity of culture from one end of the Greek world to the other, inspired by the art of Athens. The strongest and most paradoxical feature of the artistic triumph of Athens is that it was achieved at the moment of the political and economic decline of the city and the end of the Peloponnesian War when direct imports from Attica ceased.

The most typical feature of the jewellery of southern Italy in this period is a dependance on the monuments of the 'major arts', i.e. sculpture and painting, both in subject-matter and in style. The goldsmith now lost the independence which had enabled him to express himself in a fundamentally abstract manner appropriate to the decorative purpose and the small scale of the objects on which he was working. Realistic representation was either not involved at all or, if it was, the figures were adapted and arranged schematically. Now, on the other hand, the tendency was to adapt the forms and motifs of painting and sculpture. We now get, perhaps for the first time, a distinction between art and craft which certainly had not existed in the previous generation. The new development coincides perhaps with a period of stagnation in the arts which covers the last years of the 5th century BC and the early years of the 4th, the period between the great generation of Pheidias and Polycleitus, and that of Praxiteles, Scopas and Lysippus.

The new features can be seen most clearly in the very large series of incised ring bezels which became more precisely oval in shape. The commonest motif is the seated female figure shown in profile and carrying various attributes – bird, cymbals etc. The designs, especially the earlier ones, are rather provincial, lacking the precise refinement of detail, and often rather heavy. More successful are a number of examples with male or female heads in profile, like the ring from Mottola in the museum at Taranto, which dates from the 4th century BC.

Some new types of earrings were developed in

this period: the *navicella* (boat-shaped), the type with the protoma (foreparts) of a lion, and the spiral, all of which were to be very popular in Hellenistic times. The disc earrings of the period are particularly interesting; they have pendants of various kinds, including female busts, conical drops and little amphorae. Some very fine examples, with extensive use of filigree, survive. Necklaces are usually composed of fine chain or interlace, and have lion-protomas at the ends; the archaic type with pendants stamped out of gold sheet were sometimes revived.

L. Breglia has tried to distinguish the work of Apulian craftsmen and those of Campania. The study of the contents of tombs, which have in fact yielded almost all the ancient jewellery we possess, has led to the conclusion that in Magna Graecia generally earrings are almost universal but fibulae are rare; in Campania the opposite is the case and several very fine fibulae, chiefly from the cemeteries of Cumae and Teano are now in the National Museum at Naples. The chief stylistic differences between the two groups derive from the different cultural background. In Apulia the connections with Greek prototypes are more direct and the style in general is more sober and restrained; in Campania the jewellery is more eclectic, combining Greek and Etruscan motifs, and tends to be more elaborate. One is reminded of the picture of Campanian society which emerges from the accounts of ancient writers who draw attention to a deep-rooted taste for luxury and wealth. Livy (*History of Rome*, XXVI, 14) records that after the sack of Capua in the Second Punic War (211 BC) the Romans acquired 2,070 lb of gold and 31,200 lb of silver. The development of Campanian jewellery can be followed accurately from the late 5th century BC; in the course of the 4th century it becomes increasingly easy to distinguish. The chief centre of production was certainly Capua.

In Etruria the 5th century BC was a period of decline. A series of defeats, the most severe being at the battle of Cumae in 474 BC which led to the evacuation of Campania, coming on top of the revolts of the Latin peoples against their Etruscan overlords (tradition dates the expulsion of the Etruscan kings from Rome to 509 BC), and finally the invasions of the Celts in the Etruscan-occupied Po valley had vastly reduced the territory directly or immediately under Etruscan control. To a certain extent the 4th century BC saw a recovery but it was a brief one, the last before the final collapse. The crisis of the times was inevitably reflected in the art of the period. In jewellery it is obvious, especially in the lack of a creative link with contemporary Greek art which does not seem to have exerted any direct influence in Etruria for the whole of the 5th century. What we have, therefore, is a rather tired production of objects very like those of the preceding period. There are very few new forms and even these are not of great importance.

32 Pair of gold earrings. From Crispiano. 4th century BC
Museo Archeologico Nazionale, Taranto.

32   Pair of gold earrings. From Crispiano. 4th century BC. Museo Archeologico Nazionale, Taranto. Each earring has a disc decorated with filigree work consisting of a rosette composed of four concentric rings of petals framed in a wave-pattern. A female head with very fine chased detail hangs from each disc. The heads are diademed with the hair waved back from the forehead; they wear earrings and a necklace of pear-shaped pendants worked in filigree. At the sides hang chains of alternately spherical and biconical beads. Classical Greek work from Magna Graecia.

33   Gold earring. From Perugia. End of the 4th century BC or beginning of the 3rd. British Museum, London. The earring consists of an oblong convex sheet with filigree decoration from which hangs a pendant in the form of a head of a woman wearing long earrings. At the sides are pendants in the form of little amphorae. Etruscan work of the early Hellenistic period.

34   Gold ring. From Taranto. 4th century BC. Museo Archeologico Nazionale, Taranto. The oval bezel is carved in intaglio with the figure of a woman wearing a long *chiton*, girt at the waist; her hair is gathered up on the crown of her head and she wears earrings. She stands with her right arm resting on a column and she holds a wreath in her left hand. Classical Greek work from Magna Graecia.

33 Gold earring. From Perugia. End of the 4th century BC
or beginning of the 3rd. British Museum, London.

34   Gold ring. From Taranto. 4th century BC.

Towards the end of the century the use of the *bulla* became more common; in the course of the 4th and 3rd centuries it was to become very widespread either by itself or as an element of a necklace. It was then adoped by the Romans; according to Pliny this had already taken place in the time of Tarquin the Elder. From a technical point of view, the quality of the jewellery declines. Filigree and granulation practically disappear, relief-respoussé on sheet gold becomes more common; the sheet is usually very thin and the style of the reliefs rather coarse. This is the technique which is generally used in the relief *bullae* (amulets) from the 4th century onwards.

Already at the beginning of the 5th century Pindar (cited by Athenaeus) praised the objects of gold and bronze made in Etruria: 'The bronze Etruscan cup plated with gold is supreme for every purpose in the house.'

These words are clear proof of the admiration which the Greeks had for Etruscan metalwork of the archaic period; they could certainly not have been written a few decades later. The beginning of the 4th century on the other hand, saw a reversal of the process. In this period there was a real revival in the Greek areas of Italy as well as in Magna Graecia and Sicily, although they too had been declining in the second half of the 5th century. In Sicily there was the reconquest and recolonisation by Timoleon of areas occupied by the Carthaginians. We are struck by the more unified and homogeneous character of Greek culture which shows its great powers of penetration in every sphere from town-planning to practical craftsmanship, an earnest of what was to happen on an even greater scale in Hellenistic times. The Barbarians on the frontiers of the Greek world, among them the Carthaginians, the Iberians, the Scythians and the Celts, were increasingly penetrated by Greek culture.

In Etruria contacts with Greek civilisation were re-established through the colonies of Magna Graecia. Tarentum took on an increasingly important role as, to a lesser extent, did Capua. Trade with these areas became more active; goldsmiths' work was exported to Etruria, and local Etruscan work shows a close dependence on the art of Magna Graecia. The types of jewellery are also the same in both areas – necklaces, sometimes with pendants, usually of *bulla*-form, and earrings with pendants consisting of little vases or female heads. However, compared with the south Italian pieces, Etruscan work is rather provincial and secondhand, as one can see from its attempts at simplification and surface effects. The earrings made of repoussé sheet show a particular taste for hemispherical shapes in high relief; in some of the necklaces semi-precious stones and beads of glass-paste or amber become more common. Among the types of jewellery which were probably of south Italian origin is the wreath of gold leaf, usually for funerary use, which was to have a long history in Hellenistic times.

Pliny calls this type of crown or wreath the 'corona etrusca', and he also refers to the *bulla* as the 'etruscum aurum'. The funerary purpose of these wreaths is also clear from the Laws of the Twelve Tables which aimed at suppressing luxury in burial practices; they forbid 'expensive perfumes, long crowns and incense', and add that gold should not be placed in the tombs except in the case of gold-filled teeth. Cicero greatly admired this piece of legal quibbling.

The Hellenistic Period

The campaigns of Alexander the Great enormously increased the extent of the Greek world, bringing into its orbit vast territories and huge populations. The conquered territories, such as Egypt and Mesopotamia, had their own ancient civilisations; Greek culture had to assert itself in particularly difficult areas and inevitably changed in the process. This result is nowhere more obvious than in the arts; though in the end Greek form became the dominating force, it is certain that the very basis of Classical art was profoundly modified. Greek artistic expression had come into being in a society of modest proportions, the *polis*, which, because of its economic and political weakness, and for reasons of simple survival, was formed into a very closely knit and homogeneous community. The art of such a community, which from the end of the 6th century tended to a democratic form of government, was devoted not to

35 Gold ring. From Mottola. 4th century BC. Museo
Archeologico Nazionale, Taranto.

36   Gold ring. From Taranto. 4th century BC. Museo
Archeologico Nazionale, Taranto.

37 Gold bracelet. From Mottola. 4th century BC. Museo Archeologico Nazionale, Taranto.

35 Gold ring. From Mottola. 4th century BC. Museo Archeologico Nazionale, Taranto. The big oval bezel is delicately carved with a profile female head wearing her hair in the so-called 'melon' coiffure; she has a necklace and pendant earrings. Classical Greek work from Magna Craecia.

36 Gold ring. From Taranto. 4th century BC. Museo Archeologico Nazionale, Taranto. The oval bezel has an intaglio figure of a woman wearing a *chiton* which leaves one breast exposed and a mantle about her legs. She sits with her left arm resting on the back of her chair and holds a little bird in her right hand. Classical Greek work from Magna Graecia.

37 Gold bracelet. From Mottola. 4th century BC. Museo Archeologico Nazionale, Taranto. Spiral bracelet terminating in finely chased rams' heads; the collars are decorated with filigree S-spirals. Classical Greek work from Magna Graecia.

38 Gold bracelet. From Taranto. 4th—3rd century. Museo Archeologico Nazionale, Taranto. The outer surface is convex; the lions' heads are superbly chased and are joined to collars decorated with filigree leaves. Late Classical or early Hellenistic work from Magna Graecia.

38 Gold bracelet. From Taranto. 4th – 3rd century BC.
Museo Archeologico Nazionale, Taranto.

private purposes but to social and religious ends. Its best expression was always to be seen in the sanctuaries which were not only religious centres, but centres of civil life. It was the *demos*, the people, who commissioned the works of art; the work of the artist was never so democratic an activity as it was in 5th-century Athens. This is the atmosphere that is implied in the Socratic Dialogues, an atmosphere in which culture in all its aspects is not the achievement of an elite but part of the common heritage of the people. Ancient democracy, therefore, was the product of a small community and, inevitably, it could not adapt itself to a much more vast and complex world. On a different scale the same phenomenon may be seen in Rome where the Republican form of government, created for a city-state with a modest territory, collapsed under the weight of Rome's newly acquired Empire.

The rulers who emerged after the conquests of Alexander had two alternatives open to them – either to try a genuine fusion between the newly conquered peoples and the Greek element, or to follow an easier course and impose the rule of a Greek elite on the subject peoples. The former was the ambition of Alexander, who tried to bring it into effect by marrying his soldiers to Persian women and himself taking Roxane as his bride. The latter course was the one most generally chosen, and this led to a rapid decline at the very beginning of the Hellenistic period.

In this society there arose a courtly art in the service of a very tiny minority of the population. Though its Greek form remained unchanged, its content was now profoundly different. In design and purpose Hellenistic art is much closer to the art of the Achaemenid empire, which always served as the chief model for the Hellenistic kingdoms, than to that of the free city-states of Classical Greece. All this is particularly relevant to the history of jewellery. If our analysis of the historical situation is correct, we must expect a very rapid development of all those aspects of art which are closely bound up with the luxury of the court; and this, in fact, is what happened. Vast capital was now concentrated in the hands of Hellenistic kings, wealth that Greece in the 5th century had already encountered when the treasures of the Persian camp were revealed to the victors of Plataea. The campaigns of Alexander added many more astonishments of this kind. After the battle of Issus, according to Plutarch (*Alexander*, 20, 11-13), 'Alexander . . . took the chariot and the bow of Darius, and then went back. He found the Macedonians looting the enemy camp and carrying off an enormous quantity of booty despite the fact that the Persians had left most of their baggage in Damascus and had come to the battle with light equipment. For Alexander they had reserved Darius' tent with his servants and furniture and all the treasure it contained . . . When he saw the bowls, the pitchers, the bath-tubs and the scent bottles, all of gold and the finest workmanship, and smelt the heavenly aroma of the perfumes that filled the place, and when he had entered the tent, wonderful in its height and splendour and its elegant furnishings, he looked at his companions and said: "This, it seems, is what it means to be a king".'

The influence of Achaemenid culture is, as we have said, very strongly felt in the work of goldsmiths and silversmiths; there is an enormous increase in output and a return to almost entirely private purposes. The types of jewellery, the ornamental details and the style, also illustrate the same influences. One obvious feature is the increased use of stones, pearls, glass-paste, evidence of a greater interest in colour effects than in plastic form. But the fundamentally organic character of Greek art survives, absorbing these new elements and submitting them to its own formal discipline. The new production, while it has its basis in the art of the 4th century, is vastly enriched with new types and forms. In addition to the areas traditionally linked with Greece – Macedonia, Thessaly, southern Russia and Magna Graecia – there were now the new cities, capitals of Hellenistic kingdoms, of which the most important were Alexandria and Antioch. These two cities, favoured by their position as commercial centres in the trade between the Middle and Far East, monopolised the supply of precious stones. Though the actual

39 Gold spiral bracelet. From Montefortino. 4th – 3rd century BC. Museo Nazionale, Ancona.

39 Gold spiral bracelet. From Montefortino. 4th – 3rd century BC. Museo Nazionale, Ancona. The coil forms a triple spiral ending in serpents' heads. Etruscan work of the early Hellenistic period.

40 Central element of a diadem. From Crispiano. End of 4th–early 3rd century BC. Museo Archeologico Nazionale, Taranto. The gold sheet is semi-cylindrical in shape; the edge is decorated with filigree beading and wave pattern. An acanthus calyx forms the central motif, and from it spread tendrils with palmettes and bell-shaped flowers, all carried out in filigree. Early Hellenistic work from Magna Graecia.

40　Central element of a diadem. From Crispiano. End of 4th – early 3rd century BC. Museo Archeologico Nazionale, Taranto.

41 Figure of a wild goat. From Edessa. 4th—3rd century BC. Museo Archeologico Nazionale, Naples. The statuette is of solid gold; the animal stands with his head turned to one side. Greco-Persian work.

41   Figure of a wild goat. From Edessa. 4th — 3rd century
BC. Museo Archeologico Nazionale, Naples.

discoveries from these centres have been rare, there is, at least, some compensation in the very precise descriptions by contemporary writers. One of the most remarkable is that of a 3rd-century writer, Callixenus of Rhodes, preserved by Athenaeus, who gives an account of a procession of Ptolemy Philadelphus in which an enormous quantity of jewellery and silver was exhibited. As far as Antioch is concerned, it is worth noting that the capital of the Seleucid Empire was in close commercial contact with the distant territories of northern India and Bactria which were for some time part of the Empire itself. Out of these contacts came an art with a Greek basis but with Persian, Scythian and Indian elements, which expressed itself with particular effect in jewellery and goldsmith's work. But despite the various exotic elements, perhaps the most remarkable feature of the Hellenistic age is the genuine uniformity of culture in areas so different and so far from one another. The term *koine*, invented to describe the language written and spoken throughout the Hellenistic world after Alexander – a standard cosmopolitan language almost without any regional dialects – serves also as a description of other aspects of the Hellenistic world and especially its art. The jewellery produced in this period reveals a strikingly uniform artistic language, so much so that it becomes almost impossible to distinguish centres of production. It takes a very keen eye and vast experience to distinguish between a piece of jewellery made by a crafts-man in the Crimea, say, and one made in Apulia. New ideas spread very rapidly and the place of origin cannot now be established. This phenomenon is less obvious, naturally, in the major arts where one can pick out to some extent different styles, but in the case of minor craftsmanship, partly because of a deficiency in our research but chiefly because of the tendency to mass-production, it is far more difficult.

In Greece proper, impoverished as it was and reduced to the status of a Macedonian colony, we cannot expect to find a great deal of jewellery. Northern regions, Epirus, Thessaly as well as Macedonia, take on a new importance. From Thessaly, especially, comes one very remarkable group of objects which passed into the Stathatos Collection and is now in the National Museum at Athens. It is uncertain whether this jewellery should be attributed to Thessalian craftsmen or to Macedonian; in any case the two areas are very closely connected. A treasure, found by chance probably in the area of Domokos, seems to consist of objects made in the 3rd century, and it has been suggested that the circumstances of its burial were connected with the war between Rome and Perseus of Macedon around 168 BC. Among the finest pieces are belts with buckles in the form of a Hercules knot; the gold is enriched by semi-precious stones most skilfully inlaid. The Hercules knot assumes not only the function of an ornament but also that of an amulet since it was held to have magical powers. It is used not only as a belt-buckle but also as an isolated decorative element in bracelets, diadems and rings.

The treasure also includes bracelets of snake form, a motif which appears at the beginning of the Hellenistic age and goes on for thousands of years, and a series of circular medallions with busts of divinities, among them Artemis and Aphrodite, joined to a network of gold chain and serving probably to cover the breasts. The most outstanding piece is the *naiskos*, a little gold shrine, with Dionysus and a satyr, also in the Stathatos Collection in the National Museum, Athens. In all these pieces one is struck by the extensive use of semi-precious stones, especially garnets but also cornelian and sardonyx, and of glass-paste. There is now a much greater variety of techniques for working the gold, and filigree is very common. One is astonished by the extreme richness of the ornament and the taste for colour in an age so near the Classical period, and there is little doubt that Oriental, especially Persian, influence was more strongly felt in jewellery than in other branches of art.

These objects give us a good idea of the taste of Macedonian society, and that of northern Greece in general, after the death of Alexander. To the reign of Alexander himself may be attributed the find made in a tomb near Salonika; the tomb, the contents of which are now in the Metropolitan Museum, New

York, was probably that of a princess. Among the objects from the tomb are two earrings with pendants representing Ganymede snatched away by the eagle. They date from the last years of the 4th century, the period of transition between the Classical and the Hellenistic. Compared with the Thessalian find described above, they reveal the remarkable changes in style that took place in the space of a few decades. On the wealth of the Macedonian court in Hellenistic times we are all well informed by literary sources of the Roman period. The triumph celebrated by Aemilius Paullus after the battle of Pydna (168 BC) is described to us by Plutarch whose account in his life of Aemilius Paullus is particularly rich in detail (Plutarch, *Aemilius Paullus*, 32-33):

'The triumph took three days. The first day scarcely sufficed to show the statues, paintings, and colossal figures which had been captured from the enemy and were paraded on 250 carts . . . Behind the carts carrying the urns there was a column of 3,000 men carrying silver coin in 750 vessels, each weighing three talents and borne by four men. Others held silver craters, drinking horns, cups and goblets, each of them superb to look at, remarkable both for size and for the height of the relief-work . . . Behind the trumpeters were 120 sacrificial bulls with gilded horns and heads decorated with wreaths and fillets; they were brought to sacrifice by young men with bordered tunics and followed by children who carried gold and silver cups

42 Gold *naiskos*. From Thessaly. 3rd century BC. Stathatos
Collection, National Museum, Athens.

43 Part of a gold belt. From Thessaly. 3rd century BC.
Stathatos Collection, National Museum, Athens.

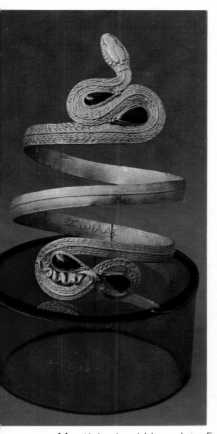

44 Pair of gold bracelets. From Thessaly. Early 3rd century BC. Benaki Museum, Athens.

42   Gold *naiskos*. From Thessaly. 3rd century BC. Stathatos Collection, National Museum, Athens. Dionysos holds a cup in his right hand and rests his left arm on the shoulder of a satyr. Hellenistic Greek.

43   Part of a gold belt. From Thessaly. 3rd century BC. Stathatos Collection, National Museum, Athens. The belt is most elaborately decorated with filigree, granulation, enamel and glass-paste. Hellenistic Greek.

45   Gold diadem. From Thessaly. First decades of the 3rd century BC. Benaki Museum, Athens.

44   Pair of gold bracelets. From Thessaly. Early 3rd century BC. Benaki Museum, Athens. These snake bracelets are decorated with incised scales; cornelian beads decorate the coils at the two ends. Hellenistic Greek.

45   Gold diadem. From Thessaly. First decades of the 3rd century BC. Benaki Museum, Athens. Ionic capitals flank the Hercules' knot in the centre which is decorated with stones and with green and blue enamel. Hellenistic Greek.

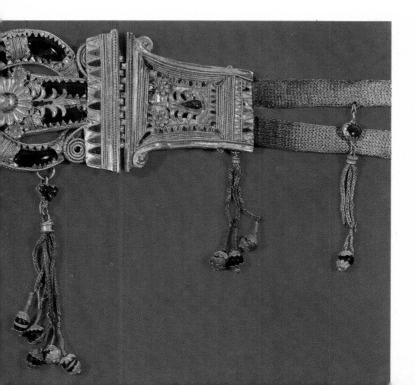

for libations. Then came the bearers of gold money, distributed like the silver in vessels each weighing three talents. There were seventy-seven of these vessels. Then came the bearers of the sacrificial cup which Aemilius had had made from ten talents of gold studded with precious stones; and others who held up for public admiration the cups known by the name Antigonid or Seleucid or Therikleian and the rest of the gold vessels which Perseus used at table. Last of all came the chariot of Perseus with his weapons and, on the weapons, his crown.'

The area which has yielded the greatest quantity of Hellenistic jewellery is southern Russia. The output here is very varied and abundant, and the jewellery was even richer and more splendid than that discovered in Thessaly. Worthy of special mention are a number of diadems with a Hercules knot made up of inlaid stones, medallions, earrings, funerary wreaths of sheet gold imitating real garlands of fruit and flowers, necklaces and bracelets. This jewellery which is comparatively little known in the West, makes the collection of the Hermitage Museum in Leningrad by far the richest in the world.

At the other end of the Greek world, in Magna Graecia, a similar phenomenon occurs. Tarentum reached the height of its power and wealth in the early years of the 3rd centruy BC, and the production of jewellery was then at its most flourishing. After the first encounter with Rome during the Pyrrhic War

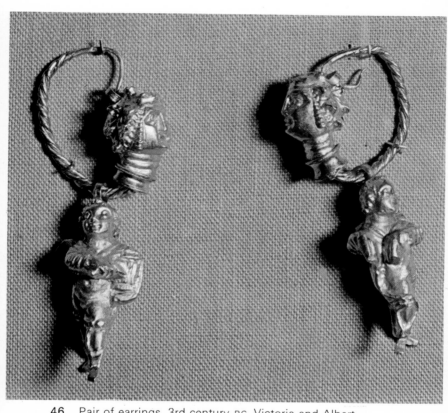

46   Pair of earrings, 3rd century BC. Victoria and Albert
Museum, London.

47 Gold medallion. From Thessaly. 3rd century BC.
Stathatos Collection, National Museum, Athens.

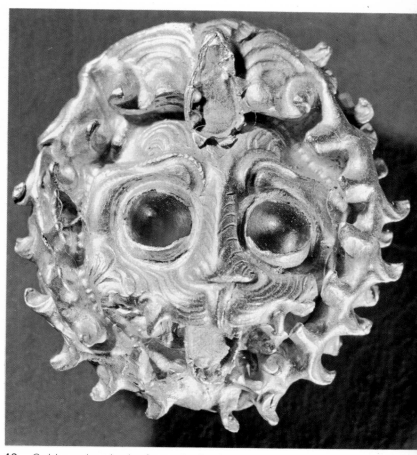

48 Gold pendant in the form of a lion's mask. From Monte
Sannace (Gioia del Colle). End of 4th — early 3rd century
BC. Museo Archeologico Nazionale, Taranto.

46   Pair of earrings. 3rd century BC. Victoria and Albert Museum, London. Spiral loops end in female heads; putti playing musical instruments hang from the loops. Hellenistic Greek.

47   Gold medallion. From Thessaly. 3rd century BC. Stathatos Collection, National Museum, Athens. A high relief roundel with a bust of Artemis is fixed at the centre of the medallion. Artemis has her hair tied on the crown of her head; she wears a *chiton* and an animal skin knotted on her right shoulder. The medallion has sixteen little rings soldered on the edge and these support a network of gold chain; at the intersection of the net there are little rosettes and medallions decorated with profile heads. Hellenistic work.

48   Gold pendant in the form of a lion's mask. From Monte Sannace (Gioia del Colle). End of 4th—early 3rd century BC. Museo Archeologico Nazionale, Taranto. The head was punched out and the details chased in; the eyes are inset with red glass and the mane is finely engraved. Early Hellenistic work from Magna Graecia.

49   Gold pendant. End of 4th or early 3rd century BC. Victoria and Albert Museum, London. Head of a goddess, probably Hera. Her hair is parted in the centre and she wears a decorated diadem. Early Hellenistic Greek.

49 Gold pendant. End of 4th or early 3rd century BC.
Victoria and Albert Museum, London.

the city was forced to surrender and suffered a severe blow to its political and military power. However, from an economic and commercial point of view, the city continued to flourish until the Second Punic War, when, after allying itself with Hannibal in 212 BC, it was conquered and sacked by the Romans three years later. The city never recovered from this terrible blow; in the pages of the Roman historians Polybius and Livy we have a description of the treasures looted from the city.

The sack of Tarentum and those of Syracuse and Capua which preceded it by a few years were the first occasions which brought great quantities of foreign works of art, especially of gold and silver, into the city. These are the years with which the moralists associate the beginning of the decline in Roman customs which the many Roman Catos were to lament so monotonously. One piece of jewellery which became increasingly common in the tombs of this period is the gold wreath or diadem. These wreaths are generally composed of sheet gold cut into the shapes of leaves and then arranged carefully on a solid support. In some cases the wreath is so fragile that it can only have had a purely funerary purpose; other examples, as Breglia observes, could also have been used as ordinary jewellery. There are, in fact, pictures on painted vases where female figures are often shown wearing wreaths of foliage. The use of a wreath or diadem with various floral elements applied to it was especially common at Tarentum not only for women but also in some cases for men, as one can see in several terracottas of the period. This 'garlando-mania' which Tarentum shared with Alexandria was still well known in later Roman times if we may judge from the fact that Juvenal describes the city as 'Crowned Tarentum'.

However it is the diadems which provide the best examples of the technical skill and artistic merit of the craftsmen. The first and best known example comes from a 3rd century tomb at Canosa (plate 51), though whether it was made there or imported from Tarentum is an open question. It was found with a silver mirror case, a jewel box, an earring and a sceptre, all of which are now in the National Museum at Taranto. The diadem consists of two curved sheets joined by a hinge in front and covered with the most minute decoration consisting of over 150 little flowers made of gold leaf and coloured enamel, glass-paste and tiny stones. Between the flowers are inserted little stems and leaves of gold, and a gold fillet with green enamel seems to bind itself round the flower stem to hold them together. It is clearly a version in precious materials of an actual floral wreath, and there is no piece of jewellery which reveals the spirit of the age better than this most intricate and skilful work with its masterly naturalistic detail. This was an age of refined but artificial culture, which became the more artificial the more it tried to be simple and

50   Pair of bracelets. 3rd century BC. Metropolitan Museum (Rogers Fund 1956), New York.

51   Gold diadem. From Canosa. 3rd century BC. Museo
Archeologico Nazionale, Taranto.

50   Pair of bracelets. 3rd century BC. Metropolitan Museum (Rogers Fund 1956), New York. Two marine divinities, a triton and a tritoness, are shown carrying figures of Eros in their arms. Early Hellenistic Greek.

51   Gold diadem. From Canosa. 3rd century BC. Museo Archeologico Nazionale, Taranto. The floral decoration contains green, white, red and blue enamels; glass-paste and semi-precious stones are used for the stamens and pistils. Vine stems are interlaced with flowers, and an enamelled strip forms a fillet binding the flowers together. Early Hellenistic work from Magna Graecia.

52   Gold wreath. From a tomb at Fondo Sperandio, Perugia. 3rd century BC. Museo Gregoriano, Vatican. This is a funerary wreath of olive-leaves with a circular boss in the centre. Etruscan work of the Hellenistic period.

53   Gold wreath. 3rd century BC. Once in the Campanari Collection, now in the British Museum, London. A rich funerary wreath of ivy leaves, delicately and precisely worked. Etruscan work of the Hellenistic period.

52   Gold wreath. From a tomb at Fondo Sperandio,
Perugia. 3rd century BC. Museo Gregoriano, Vatican.

53 Gold wreath. 3rd century BC. Once in the Campanari
Collection, now in the British Museum, London.

spontaneous. One thinks of the contemporary poetry of Theocritus with its improbable shepherds and Arcadians. The style reminds one of the Mannerism of the late *cinquecento*; Cellini would certainly have admired a work of this kind.

Disc-earrings with pendants, of a type which first appeared in the preceding century, continued to be made at Tarentum. The Oriental details became more and more intricate, and granulation came back into fashion. Pendants, sometimes enamelled, take on a variety of forms. Apart from the inverted pyramidal shapes and female heads we get birds, figures of Eros or of Ganymede, little amphorae and so on. In Campania, as we have already seen, there are no earrings from the area round Capua, but there are some from the coastal region, at Cumae. This has been explained, and rightly, as a result of the flourishing trade between Tarentum and Naples in the 3rd century.

The rings with oval or circular gold bezel are an important group. They illustrate again the taste for minute detail such as we have already seen in Tarentine work. The figured subjects, especially on the circular bezels, tend to become smaller and smaller, so that the superb detail is often hard to see. Other typical objects of the 4th century are earrings and necklaces of gold interlace, plain or with pendants, and necklaces with inlaid stones and glass-paste. The Hercules knot sometimes crops up, as on an example in the Taranto Museum, but there are no stone inlays of the kind found on examples from Thrace and southern Russia; instead we find filigree ornament. In Campania there is an outstanding series of fibulae, generally of leech-type which continued from the preceding century, and a series of rings with engraved circular bezels.

In the century after the Second Punic War, Magna Graecia continued to produce the standard types of jewellery which were repeated endlessly with very little variation or inspiration. The technique is much poorer and the style mechanical and rigid. The cities lost their political importance, and their population and economy generally declined; their territories became the ranches of wealthy senators and knights. In Campania the position was somewhat different because the agricultural and commercial importance of the area enabled it to preserve a colourful independence down to Augustan times. But the old cities of Cumae and Capua lost their importance, while Puteoli (Pozzuoli) came to prominence as one of the chief ports of the Mediterranean.

In Etruria the decline was even more rapid. In the course of the 3rd century the last cities fell into Rome's hands and the upper classes left their possessions to move into the city. The decline in population is astonishing; in a few decades one of the most flourishing parts of ancient Italy became an uninhabited and malarial marshland. Nevertheless, jewellery went on being made in the 3rd century in the style of the previous century; there was nothing in the way of important or notable differences, except that technique and quality gradually declined. As Mansuelli has said, 'This output cannot conceal its basic mass-production; it comes from the workshop rather than the craftsman. One feels that the detail corresponds neither to reality nor to the taste of the artist; it has become meaningless and superficial. Jewellery (and indeed all craftsmanship) declines with mass-production . . . The goldsmith or silversmith is no longer able to stamp his work, not with the mark of his individual personality, (for this is very rare indeed in the work of craftsmen) but with the distinctive expression of the world in which he lives and for which he works.'

While Italy declined, the eastern Hellenistic centres, Antioch and Alexandria, grew steadily in importance. In these years the meeting between these centres and the Italian world, exhausted and now completely under Rome's rule, laid the foundations of a new culture which may be called the Hellenistic-Roman.

The Roman Period

One can only speak of Roman art in the last hundred years of the Republican period. Before that there was no artistic output with its own characteristics to which one could give such a name. From its first very

54 Gold *bulla*. 3rd century BC. Once in the Pourtalès
Collection, now in the British Museum, London.

55 Gold earring. Provenance unknown. 3rd century BC.
Metropolitan Museum, New York.

54   Gold *bulla*. 3rd century BC. Once in the Pourtalès Collection, now in the British Museum, London. Part of a necklace, decorated with a repoussé relief showing three figures seated round a large vessel — probably a ritual scene. Etruscan work of the Hellenistic period.

55   Gold earring. Provenance unknown. 3rd century BC. Metropolitan Museum, New York. The convex gold sheet is decorated with rosettes and beading; the pendant consists of a female head with hair parted in the centre. Etruscan work of the Hellenistic period.

56   Gold ring. From Capua. 1st century BC. Museo Archeologico Nazionale, Naples. The oval bezel is of paler gold and is decorated with a male portrait head in profile to the left; the ring is signed by a certain Herakleidas. Scholars date the ring variously between the 3rd and the 1st century BC. Roman.

57   Solid gold disc. From Pompeii. 3rd century BC. Museo Archeologico Nazionale, Naples. The figure of a woman, carved in sardonyx, is inlaid in the centre of the disc; she is holding a drinking horn in her left hand and a serpent in the other. Roman work of the Hellenistic period.

56 Gold ring. From Capua. 1st century BC. Museo Archeologico Nazionale, Naples.

57　Solid gold disc. From Pompeii. 3rd century BC.
Museo Archeologico Nazionale, Naples.

modest beginnings Rome was quickly absorbed into the Etruscan orbit. It is possible that craftsmen's workshops existed there in the Orientalising period and they may have produced jewellery. Rome, in fact, very probably presented the same appearance in art and culture as Palestrina; but this is only hypothesis, and direct evidence is completely lacking. The period that followed is beginning to be better known; recent excavation, especially in the area of S. Ombono, has brought to light archaic material including temple-terracottas which cannot be distinguished from contemporary Etruscan work. We know, furthermore, from Pliny that at the end of the 6th century an artist of Veii named Vulca was called in to decorate the temple of Jupiter Capitolinus; Vulca's work is probably to be recognised in the big terracotta sculptures found at Veii which are now in the Villa Giulia Museum. Even later it is difficult to distinguish a characteristically 'Roman' production; for a long time, even after the expulsion of the Tarquins, the city remained culturally dependent on Etruria. Later still, at the end of the Classical period and in the early Hellenistic, Rome was part of that vast artistic *koine* which extended from Etruria to Campania. Only when the Italian peninsula as a whole was in decline after the Punic and Eastern Wars do we begin to see signs of some originality appearing in every sphere; in literature, especially in the circle of the Scipios, in architecture and, less clearly, in sculpture and painting. What had happened in the meantime? Rome had for the first time come into direct contact with the great Hellenistic kingdoms. Their defeat had produced an enormous influx of capital into the city which, in a very few decades, was transformed from a modest city-state into the economic and financial capital of the Mediterranean. This rapid and violent transformation saw the beginnings of that prolonged crisis which continued from the Gracchi to Octavian and eventually brought about the creation of the Roman Empire.

In the field of art a similar phenomenon occurred. As a result of the looting of works of art, Rome became a vast museum which gathered together all the best work that the Hellenic world had produced. After the objects came the men, and soon Rome was invaded by 'Greeklings' – architects, sculptors, painters, goldsmiths, gem engravers. The city was not prepared for an invasion on this scale. There were, it is true, enlightened men like Flamininus, the victor of Cynoscephalae, and above all Scipio Aemilianus and Laelius, who understood the need to prepare the Roman ruling class for its new duty as the elite of the world and who tried by every means in their power to carry this out. But the majority of the senatorial aristocracy was unequal to the task. It is clear that they did not get beyond a somewhat hypocritical moralising when they thought about art. We see, for example, what Pliny the Elder, a man of wide culture, thought of gem collecting which had become increasingly popular from the 1st century BC onwards. The passage which concerns us reads as follows:

'However, it was this victory of Pompey over Mithridates that made fashion veer to pearls and gemstones. The victories of Lucius Scipio and of Cn. Manlius had done the same for chased silver, garments of cloth of gold, and dining-couches inlaid with bronze, and that of Mummius for Corinthian bronzes and paintings . . . [Pompey] in this third triumph which he celebrated over the pirates . . . carried in the procession a gaming board, complete with a set of pieces, the board being made of two precious minerals and measuring three feet broad and four feet long . . . ; three gold dining-couches; enough gold vessels inlaid with gems to fill nine display stands; three gold figures of Minerva, Mars and Apollo respectively; thirty-three pearl crowns; a square mountain of gold with deer, lions and every variety of fruit on it, and a golden vine entwined around it; and a grotto of pearls, on the top of which there was a sundial. There was also a portrait of Pompey rendered in pearls.' At this point the writer cannot refrain from the following outburst: ' . . . that portrait so pleasing, with the handsome growth of hair swept back from the forehead, the portrait of that noble head revered throughout the world – that portrait, I say, that portrait was rendered in pearls! Here it was austerity that was defeated and extravagance that more truly

58 Gold snake-bracelet. Provenance unknown. 1st century BC. Museo Archeologico Nazionale, Naples.

59 Gold snake-bracelet. 1st century AD. Museo
Archeologico Nazionale, Naples.

58   Gold snake-bracelet. Provenance unknown. 1st century BC. Museo Archeologico Nazionale, Naples. The spiral is of plain flat gold sheet while the head and tail are decorated with incised scales. The head is modelled, and the eyes were originally inlaid with stones. Roman.

59   Gold snake-bracelet. 1st century AD. Museo Archeologico Nazionale, Naples. Bracelet of solid gold with three coils; the decoration is confined to scales incised at the two ends. The head is finely modelled. Roman.

60   Gold necklace. From Pompeii. 1st century BC. — 1st century AD. Museo Archeologico Nazionale, Naples. The necklace is decorated with nine rectangular emeralds and eight oval mother-of-pearl beads. There is another emerald inset in the disc-shaped buckle. Roman.

61   Large gold ring. From Pompeii. 1st century AD. Museo Archeologico Nazionale, Naples. The oval bezel is incised with the standing figure of a god, probably Zeus; his head is wreathed and he holds a patera (shallow dish) in his left hand. Roman work of the early Imperial period.

60   Gold necklace. From Pompeii. 1st century BC. — 1st
century AD. Museo Archeologico Nazionale, Naples.

61 Large gold ring. From Pompeii. 1st century AD. Museo Archeologico Nazionale, Naples.

celebrated its triumph. Never, I think, could his surname "the Great" have survived among the stalwarts of that age had he celebrated his first triumph in this fashion.'

He goes on for a good sixteen lines interspersed with questions and shocked exclamations. And all because of a portrait in precious stones. How much more sensible and intelligent is the speech of Tiberius to the senate in which he criticises the aediles who had proposed to introduce sumptuary legislation which they would probably be the first to infringe, and with them the whole of the senatorial class which was much given to empty moralising. This is Tacitus' account (*Annals*, iii, 53) of the emperor's words:

'Which form of extravagance shall I prohibit first or cut down to the standard of the old days? Is it the vast size of our country houses? The number and varied nationality of our slaves? The piles of gold and silver? The masterpieces of painting and bronze sculpture? The rich clothes worn by men and women alike? Or that especially feminine luxury which sends our wealth to foreign and even hostile lands to buy precious stones?

'I know these things are denounced at dinner-table and other gatherings, and that restriction is urged. But if a law were passed, and penalties established, these same people would cry out that the state was being turned upside down; that all outstanding citizens were being threatened with ruin, all citizens alike with prosecutions . . . The many laws passed by our ancestors and those of the Emperor Augustus have given luxury a surer footing; the former have passed into oblivion and the latter – which is more shameful – have been completely ignored . . . Why then was frugality once the rule? Because everyone exercised self-restraint; because we were citizens of a single city and because the temptations were not so great when we ruled only in Italy. Foreign conquests have taught us to squander what belongs to others; civil war has made us wasteful even of our own.'

From the passage of Pliny cited earlier we can imagine the vast quantity of jewellery imported into Rome and later on manufactured there. We have only a very limited picture of the objects themselves chiefly because the funerary customs of the Romans, at least in the Republican period, remained comparatively simple – and archaeology, as everyone knows, lives by its tombs. It is only very rarely that we find valuable jewellery in graves. The best examples, therefore, are probably lost for ever. But we do have a certain amount, the most important group being that discovered in the towns buried by Vesuvius, especially Pompeii and Herculaneum. The finds are generally of modest quality, such as one would expect to find in a small provincial town.

We know that in Rome there were many goldsmith's shops, some on the Via Sacra. From ancient writers, and especially from inscriptions we are informed about the different specialised crafts: *caelatores* (metal-chasers), *brattearii* (makers of sheet gold), *auratores* or *inauratores* (gilders) and *margaritarii* (pearl-traders). Some idea of the activities of these craftsmen may be got from sculptures, generally of a funerary character, which represent the goldsmith at work; one of the most interesting documents is the frieze with figures of Eros as goldsmiths from the House of the Vettii at Pompeii. We have as well the description of the workshop set up by Verres at Syracuse to adapt the various works of art he had stolen. Cicero's speeches against Verres are, indeed, a real mine of information about the arts in late Hellenistic times and especially about the work of the goldsmith and silversmith to which the notorious praetor was particularly partial. 'When he had got together such a large number of *emblemata* [relief medallions generally of silver] that he had left hardly any in circulation, he set up a vast workshop in the palace at Syracuse. Then he ordered all the craftsmen, makers of vases and reliefs, to be publicly summoned though he already had a large number on his staff. He then shut them all up, this vast number of men, and for eight months there was no shortage of work although they made only gold vessels. The *emblemata* removed from sacrificial dishes and censers were so skilfully adapted to cups and gold vases that you would think they had been intended for them. The same praetor who now tells you that he was responsible

62   Gold necklace. From Pompeii. 1st century BC. — 1st
century AD. Museo Archeologico Nazionale, Naples.

63 Gold earring. 1st century BC. — 1st century AD. Museo
Archeologico Nazionale, Naples.

62   Gold necklace. From Pompeii. 1st century BC — 1st century AD. Museo Archeologico Nazionale, Naples. The necklace consists of a series of little ivy-leaves with the veins strongly marked. Large central bead. Roman.

63   Gold earring. 1st century BC. — 1st century AD. Museo Archeologico Nazionale, Naples. A little figure of Eros is attached to the large loop of the earring; he wears a necklace knotted on his chest. Roman.

64   Large lamp with two nozzles, made of gold sheet. From Pompeii. 1st century BC. Museo Archeologico Nazionale, Naples. The body of the lamp is decorated with repoussé leaves and flowers. On the handle is a large leaf. Roman.

65   Part of a gold bracelet. From Herculaneum. 1st century AD. Museo Archeologico Nazionale, Naples. The bracelet is composed of two curved sections each ending in a lion's head; geometric patterns are incised on the gold, and there is a central stamped bead. Roman.

64 Large lamp with two nozzles, made of gold sheet. From Pompeii. 1st century BC. Museo Archeologico Nazionale, Naples.

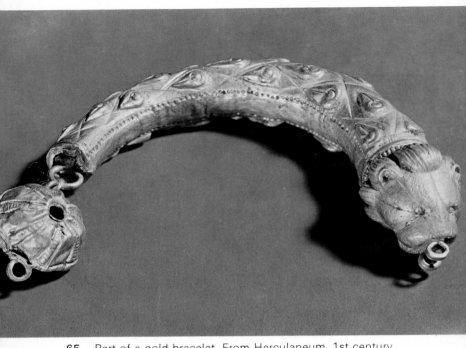

65 Part of a gold bracelet. From Herculaneum. 1st century AD. Museo Archeologico Nazionale, Naples.

for the preservation of peace in Sicily used to spend most of the day sitting in his workshop, dressed in a dark tunic and a mantle.'

The late Hellenistic tradition of southern Italy and Etruria lasted into the Republican period. Roman taste was perhaps rather closer to the Etruscan, with a preference for smooth and spherical surfaces; a new type of bracelet appeared, consisting of a double row of gold semicircles arranged in pairs. The earrings of the period have a similar appearance. The most common type of earring, however, is the one with beads, either singly or in bunches. The last variety were called 'crotalia' because of the jingling sound made when the beads rattled against one another. The commonest piece of jewellery, worn by both men and women, was the ring. Sometimes it was very simple and made of cheap metal, generally iron; sometimes it was much richer, made of gold with an intaglio sealstone of sardonyx or jasper or a gold intaglio bezel. The types belong to the Hellenistic tradition. The gold ring was for a long time the privilege of a class. In the Republican period it could be worn only by men of senatorial rank; at the beginning of the Empire it was the exclusive privilege of the knights, but later its use became widespread. Among men the custom of wearing one or sometimes many rings is clear from the funerary sculpture of the Republican period. Hannibal obtained vast numbers of rings by removing them from the bodies of Romans who had been slain at the disastrous battle of Cannae.

Another Hellenistic type of jewellery in use is the snake bracelet; a ring of the same form now makes its appearance and there are a number of very fine examples with the snake's eyes inset with tiny stones. The use of the *bulla*, which was Etruscan in origin, was now very widespread; all the children wore one round their necks, with frequently a little crescent moon as a pendant on a necklace. The latter is an amulet with very similar function to the horn of gold or coral which is used today in southern Italy. Necklaces in general show few innovations; chains, with or without pendants, are common, as are bands, often inset with semi-precious stones. Although the types of jewellery are generally the same, taste, as we have seen, was a good deal different and related most closely to the late Etruscan. The chief characteristics are greater simplicity, the abandonment of the miniaturist technique, and a preference for large plain surfaces and for brightly coloured stones.

There was very little change in quality in the early years of the Empire, but the quantity increased; the taste for ostentatious richness, often a very vulgar taste, became widespread. Rich freedmen are the chief representatives of the new society, and ancient literature has preserved an immortal picture of one of them in Trimalchio and his wealthy spouse Fortunata (Petronius, *Satyricon*, lxvii):

'So in she [Fortunata] came with her skirt tucked

up under a yellow sash to show her cerise petticoat underneath, as well as her twisted anklets and gold-embroidered slippers. Wiping her hands on a handkerchief which she carried round her neck, she took her place on the couch on which Scintilla Habinnas' wife was reclining. She kissed her. "Is it really you?" she said, clapping her hands together.'

It soon got to the point when Fortunata took the bracelets from her great fat arms and showed them to the admiring Scintilla. In the end she even undid her anklets and her gold hair net, which she said was pure gold. Trimalchio noticed this; he had it all brought to him, and commented:

'A woman's chains, you see. This is the way us poor fools get robbed. She must have six and a half pounds on her. Still, I've got a bracelet myself, made up from the one-tenth per cent offered to Mercury – and it weighs not an ounce less than ten pounds.'

Finally, for fear he might appear a liar, he even had some scales brought in and had them passed round to test the weight. Scintilla was no better. From round her neck she took a little gold locket, which she called her 'lucky box', took from it two *crotalia* (earrings with jangling beads) and gave them to Fortunata to look at.

'A present from my good husband,' she said, 'and no one had a finer set.'

'Hey!' said Habinnas, 'you cleaned me out to buy you a glass bean. Honestly, if I had a daughter, I'd cut her little ears off. If there weren't any women, everything would be dirt cheap.'

About a century later Lucian, too, attacked the extravagance of Roman women, and in doing so he described some of the jewellery which is very much the same as it was before—earrings with beads, snake bracelets and so on. 'What can one say of their other fancies which cost more still? On their earrings are stones worth many talents, on their wrists and arms gold snakes which ought to be real live ones! On their heads crowns enriched with all the jewels of India; precious necklaces round their necks. The gold goes right down to their feet and there are bangles around their ankles. Oh, would that it were an iron chain round their legs!'

From the end of the 2nd century AD Roman art underwent a process of transformation which became increasingly marked in the course of the 3rd century AD and in the end completely changed its character. With Diocletian and the Tetrarchy the fundamentally organic and realistic forms of Greek art were abandoned, giving place to a totally different artistic experience. The 'late antique' culture takes its place and with it the beginning of the Medieval.

The new phenomenon does not take the same form throughout the vast area of the Roman Empire. It is first seen, curiously enough, in the eastern provinces which were the most thoroughly Hellenised. This is to be explained by the influence exerted by peoples of

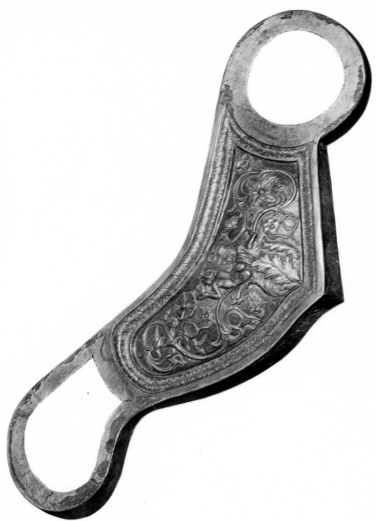

66   Part of a couch end *(pulvinum)*. From Bosco Marengo.
2nd century AD. Museo d'Antichità, Turin.

66   Part of a couch end *(pulvinum)*. From Bosco Marengo. 2nd century AD. Museo d'Antichità, Turin. Silver sheet with gilded reliefs, forming part of the decoration of a couch. The decoration consists of floral scrolls surrounding the figure of a Maenad. Roman work of the Imperial period.

67   Gold snake-bracelet. 1st — 4th century AD. Victoria and Albert Museum, London. The bracelet has three coils and terminates at either end in a serpent's head with scaly skin. Roman Imperial period.

68   Gold earring. From Granada. 2nd — 3rd century AD. British Museum, London. The earring consists of a disc decorated with a rosette, a rectangular element with a figure of Eros, and a pelta (small shield in the shape of a half-moon) with pendants. Roman Imperial period.

67 Gold snake-bracelet. 1st – 4th century AD. Victoria and Albert Museum, London.

Parthian stock and especially by the Sassanian rulers who succeeded the Arsacid kings in the 3rd century. The Arsacids had always preserved a Greek veneer and loved to speak of themselves as 'philhellenes' as part of their anti-Roman policy. The Sassanians, on the other hand, linked themselves directly with the Achaemenid kings who had ruled before Alexander, and they renounced their cosmopolitan Greek past in favour of a Persian nationalism. The rise of nationalistic feeling in Gaul, Egypt and Palmyra is one of the most important disruptive elements in the Roman Empire. From the point of view of art, the result is a strong anti-Classical tendency. Oriental modes of expression gain in importance and in the end exert profound influence throughout the Empire; one thinks particularly of the taste for overloaded jewellery of the kind to be seen on Palmyrene funerary busts. Another element, long in existence but only now becoming widespread, is what may be called the 'Barbarian' element. It is particularly important for our study because it has a very deep influence on the minor arts, particularly jewellery. As Rostovzev has shown, the main influence is the art of the Sarmatian peoples who developed their power in the 2nd century AD at the expense of the Scythian peoples of southern Russia. They brought with them the ancient art of the steppes, which they developed and, in a sense, recreated. Under the Scythians this art had been almost transformed by Greek elements.

68 Gold earring. From Granada. 2nd — 3rd century AD. British Museum, London.

These then are the new artistic forms which enter the Roman world in the wake of invaders, and constitute one of the vital elements in the creation of the art of the early Middle Ages. How are these changes represented in Roman society at the beginning of the 3rd century AD? The last sparks of the Hellenistic tradition disappeared in a production of rather poor quality; its lack of inspiration is to be seen in the increasingly frequent use of coins as ornaments in jewellery. Mechanical mass-production took the place of the inventive tradition of craftsmanship. A similar phenomenon can be seen in our own day; the crisis in our modern civilisation is, indeed, not unlike that of the ancient world, and it is reflected in small things.

There are, however, new technical and formal elements. One of the most important, called '*opus interrasile*', is probably of Syrian origin and became widespread in the 3rd century. It is, in effect, a lacelike treatment of the surface of the jewellery in the openwork technique which is particularly adapted to making arabesques and abstract ornament rather than realistic detail. It implies the rejection of 'plastic' or 'tactile' form in favour of visual effects. The same phenomenon can be seen in sculpture where the relief is no longer conceived in three-dimensional plastic form but is achieved by cutting into the surface of the marble with a drill, in what may be called a 'negative' technique.

In addition to these Oriental elements, in the 4th century AD we have typically Barbarian features, among them the use of stones, gems and glass-paste which are used solely for their colour, while the gold is reduced simply to a mounting. This contrasts strongly with Hellenistic jewellery where the stones were skilfully used as part of an organic design.

At this point our account may be considered at an end. With the appearance of these revolutionary influences, the Classical period, even in its widest sense of Greek and Roman, may be considered closed. Certain elements of Classical art survived into Byzantine and Carolingian times, and even later, but, torn from their context and lacking their original *raison d'être*, they must be considered for what they were – the miserable survivors of a great shipwreck. The distinguishing elements of the new culture that was now in the process of formation must be sought elsewhere.

LIST OF ILLUSTRATIONS   Page